Emily Mason Teaches You to Think

JOLIE WHEATON

Copyright © 2014 Jolie Wheaton.

All rights reserved. No part of this book may be used or reproduced by any means, graphic, electronic, or mechanical, including photocopying, recording, taping or by any information storage retrieval system without the written permission of the publisher except in the case of brief quotations embodied in critical articles and reviews.

WestBow Press books may be ordered through booksellers or by contacting:

WestBow Press
A Division of Thomas Nelson & Zondervan
1663 Liberty Drive
Bloomington, IN 47403
www.westbowpress.com
1 (866) 928-1240

Because of the dynamic nature of the Internet, any web addresses or links contained in this book may have changed since publication and may no longer be valid. The views expressed in this work are solely those of the author and do not necessarily reflect the views of the publisher, and the publisher hereby disclaims any responsibility for them.

Any people depicted in stock imagery provided by Thinkstock are models, and such images are being used for illustrative purposes only. Certain stock imagery © Thinkstock.

ISBN: 978-1-4908-6453-2 (sc)
ISBN: 978-1-4908-6454-9 (hc)
ISBN: 978-1-4908-6452-5 (e)

Library of Congress Control Number: 2014922986

Printed in the United States of America.

WestBow Press rev. date: 1/6/2015

Scripture quotations taken from the New American Standard Bible®, Copyright © 1960, 1962, 1963, 1968, 1971, 1972, 1973, 1975, 1977, 1995 by The Lockman Foundation. Used by permission. (www.Lockman.org)

Scripture quotations taken from the Holy Bible, New Living Translation, Copyright © 1996, 2004. Used by permission of Tyndale House Publishers, Inc., Wheaton, Illinois 60189. All rights reserved.

Scripture taken from the *Amplified Bible*, copyright © 1954, 1958, 1962, 1964, 1965, 1987 by The Lockman Foundation. Used by permission.

Scripture taken from the Holy Bible, NEW INTERNATIONAL VERSION®. Copyright © 1973, 1978, 1984 by Biblica, Inc. All rights reserved worldwide. Used by permission. NEW INTERNATIONAL VERSION® and NIV® are registered trademarks of Biblica, Inc. Use of either trademark for the offering of goods or services requires the prior written consent of Biblica US, Inc.

Dedication

I would like to dedicate this book to my parents, Lynn McWhorter and Garlan Moreland. They have always believed in me and supported me. They are two of the most creative, caring, and generous people I know. Thank you, Mom and Dad, for teaching me to live from my heart.

Introduction

I grew up asking questions, especially questions about God. I wanted to know who He was, and where He was, and what He thought. I had an unquenchable desire to know Him and to understand Him. My mother was often the one to answer my questions. One of the most important answers she ever gave was in the form of a question: "Do you believe God loves you in your heart?"

I remember standing there in our avocado green 1970s kitchen thinking, *Yes. Yes, I do believe God loves me in my heart.* In that moment, it seemed that all of my questions had found their answers.

As I have gotten older, I have had the opportunity to ask that question again and again. "I really messed up. Do I still believe God loves me in my heart?" "Wow! Missed the mark there. Do I still believe God loves me in my heart?" "Not a perfect mother, a perfect wife, a perfect daughter or sister or friend. Do I still believe God loves me in my heart?"

And the answer, of course, is always His truth. Yes, I still believe God loves me in my heart. It is this belief in God's love that has caused me to write this book. It is the belief that if we are certain of His perfect love, we will feel safe in His love, and when we feel safe in His love, we will make the best decisions. That urges me to share these stories with you. These stories are written from the perspective of a creative, delightful eight year old, but they are the same stories we all live every day. I believe that just like Emily, we all need a little practice choosing our thoughts. We all need to know the sweet, tender loving kindness of our Father. We all need His reassuring Word and His presence. We all need to be certain that God loves us in our hearts.

With love and lots of thoughts worth thinking,

Jolie

Contents

First Things First: A Little Note from Emily ... xi

Lesson 1: Why Do I Need to Choose My Thoughts? ... 1

Lesson 2: How Can I Know God When I Can't Even See Him? ... 8

Lesson 3: How Do I Know God Loves Me? ... 20

Lesson 4: Seeing Yourself the Way God Sees You ... 27

Lesson 5: When Choosing Your Thoughts Is *Not* the Best Choice ... 43

Lesson 6: What to Do When You Feel Lonely ... 53

Lesson 7: What to Do When You Feel Discouraged ... 59

Lesson 8: Uh-oh: What to Do When You Make a Mistake and Feel Guilty! ... 68

Lesson 9: What to Do When You Don't Know What to Do ... 79

Lesson 10: What to Do When You're Worried ... 91

Lesson 11: What to Do When You Feel Jealous ... 99

Lesson 12: What to Do When Someone Hurts Your Feelings ... 109

Conclusion ... 119

First Things First: A Little Note from Emily

My name is Emily, and I am eight years old. I have a favorite pair of tennis shoes, a dog named Roxy, a parakeet, and a stick of gum I'm saving for a special occasion.

This is *my* book on how to think. I'm pretty much an expert at this point because, like I said, I'm eight. So I've been practicing forever!

What do *you* think about? Do you think that what you think about is important? My mom says it's super important. She says that when you choose your thoughts, you choose your life. Sometimes I don't feel like I choose my thoughts. Sometimes I feel like they're just there, inside of me.

What do you think?

See? I asked you, and you had a thought, didn't you? You probably didn't even know it was there until I asked you, right? Well, that's just it. Thoughts are sneaky! That's why Mom's always saying, "Choose your thoughts, choose your life, Emily." Every now and then, I get a little tired of hearing that. And when I tell my mom that, she tells me to choose my thoughts ... *again*!

Okay, let's cover first things first. Do you have a place you can go that's just for you? It doesn't have to be big. It doesn't even have to be yours. It can be a closet or a bathroom or even a table with a blanket over it.

My tree house is my quiet place. My dad built it just for me! He wanted me to have a special place that was all my own. It's okay if you don't have a tree house. You can pretend. Sometimes I even pretend my tree house is not a tree house. I pretend it's other things. I pretend it's a castle, a cave, a store, or an office. One time I imagined it was a submarine.

The important thing is to have a place that makes you feel safe and happy, a place where you can just be you! I like being me.

Do you like being you? Even that has to do with choosing your thoughts. You think thoughts about yourself all day long. In fact, they are some of the most important thoughts you think.

After you find your space, you're ready to learn how to think. Choosing your thoughts takes practice because, like I said, thoughts are sneaky. They creep up on you when you don't even know they're there, and then—*wham!*—they're in your head. But that's exactly why I'm here—to teach you how to think. Don't worry. It's really pretty easy once you know you're doing it, once you know you're thinking. See? You're *thinking* about *thinking* right now. Good job!

This book is full of all kinds of thoughts for you to choose. I put my whole entire list of "Thoughts Worth Thinking" in this book. Thoughts worth thinking are keepers. They're the thoughts you *want* to think. All of the thoughts worth thinking (I call them TWTs, for short) came straight out of the Bible, so you can be sure they are God's truth for you. I even give you the verses so you can go and look them up for yourself!

The Bible tells us all about God and how He thinks. Did you know that God wants us to think like Him? That's why we have to choose our thoughts. I put in some of my own real-life stories, and I left you space to add some of yours.

Like I said, don't worry. It's easier than you think! See? There it is again, that word *think*. Thinking is so important.

It's time to get started with Lesson Number One. Be sure to write on all of the pages, and don't forget to do all of the activities. They are super fun. You can even make up your own.

See you on the next page!

Lesson 1

Why Do I Need to Choose My Thoughts?

(BTW, most of the lessons in this book come from my own curious questions. This one is from a conversation I had with my parents one night at dinner.)

This story starts with one of my curious questions. Curious questions are just questions I have sometimes, questions that don't seem to have an easy answer. On this particular occasion, I was wondering why I needed to choose my thoughts. I mean, what difference did it make anyway? I don't think about thinking. The thoughts just show up! How could I choose them even if I wanted to? When I start wondering about a curious question like that, I won't stop until I have the answer.

I decided to ask Mom and Dad while we were having dinner. It was meat loaf (sounds gross but tastes *delicious!*), mashed potatoes, and green beans.

"Um, I have one of my curious questions," I told my parents.

"Great, Punkin. I love your curious questions!" Dad sat back in his chair and waited.

"Well …" I took a breath. "I have been wondering why it is so important that I choose my thoughts."

"Good question!" Dad clapped his hands. (He always does that when I ask one of my curious questions.) "Here is my best answer. You have to choose your thoughts because your thoughts have a lot to do with how your day's gonna go," he explained.

Mom nodded. "And that has a lot to do with how your *life's* gonna go," she added.

"I don't get it," I said. "What does thinking have to do with how my day goes?"

"Because when you change the way you see things, you change your thoughts," Mom told me.

I felt more confused.

"Okay … I've got it!" Mom smiled. "Remember when you first tried green beans?" She gave me that look she gets whenever she is about to launch into a long explanation of something she finds extremely interesting and exciting.

I looked down at my plate at the little mountain of green beans all piled up next to the bigger mountain of mashed potatoes and sighed. I knew what was coming. "No, I don't think so."

"Well, I do." Dad grinned and looked at Mom. "You spit green beans in your mother's face!" They both laughed.

"Oh," I giggled. "I guess I didn't like them?"

"No, ma'am. You absolutely did not." Mom squished her face up like a baby. "Blah!" She pretended to be a baby pushing away food.

"Well, I love green beans now," I said proudly.

"Yes." Mom tapped her forehead with her finger. "That's because you chose your thoughts."

Here comes the long-explanation part.

"But I was a baby," I argued. "I didn't know how to choose my thoughts."

"We helped you," Dad explained. "Mommy kept offering you green beans every night until finally you tried them again."

"And then you decided that you *loved* them!" Mom smiled and raised her eyebrows. "See?"

"But how is that choosing my thoughts?" I did not see. None of what they were saying was making any sense to me.

"Well, let me try again." Dad squinted and rubbed his knuckles across his chin. "You took a chance and thought about those green beans in a different way." He stopped talking and looked at me. "You know what I mean?"

"You mean that because I kept trying the green beans, I was choosing my thoughts?" I asked.

"Exactly," Mom nodded. "And choosing your thoughts changed your life because now you know how much you love green beans!" She gets so excited when she thinks she has made her point.

"What if you'd never tried the green beans again?" Dad asked as I took an extra large spoonful from the bowl in the middle of the table.

"I would have missed out!" I patted my tummy. "And that would have been sad." I made a sad face. We all laughed at that. "Okay, okay. I think you have convinced me. From now on, I am going to choose my thoughts. I don't want to miss out on anything God has for me!"

Something to Think About

"We are taking every thought captive to the obedience of Christ." (2 Cor. 10:5 New American Standard Bible, NASB)

In My Own Words

I can choose my thoughts and line them up with Jesus'.

Something Fun to Do

This activity will require a tiny bit of liquid dish soap and a bathtub or a sink.

1. Fill up the tub or the sink with nice warm water.
2. Add a few drops of liquid dish soap. You won't need much.
3. Swirl the water around if you want to, and watch the bubbles fill up the whole surface of the water.
4. Now try to capture the bubbles! Bring all of them to one corner of the sink or bathtub. I make mountains with my bubbles.
5. Once all of the bubbles are captured, you will have a little island of bubbles on top of the smooth surface of the water.

Capturing those bubbles wasn't easy, was it? Sometimes they pop up somewhere else! Sometimes they slip right through your fingers! Well, our thoughts are the same way. Remember what I always say: thoughts are sneaky!

The Bible tells us to take our thoughts captive to the obedience of Christ. Do you know what that means? You took the bubbles captive when you captured them and put them all in one corner of your sink or bathtub.

When we take our thoughts captive to the obedience of Jesus, we choose to think about what Jesus has done for us and that He has given us a perfect relationship with God through His obedience on the cross. Instead of thinking about our disappointments or our fears, we can think about God's promises.

As a child of God, you can live your life knowing that God loves you and is with you. You can trust Him because you know He only has good plans for you.

Choose Your Thoughts

The next time you find yourself worrying or feeling afraid or alone, remember how you captured the bubbles. Just like you captured the bubbles, you can capture your thoughts by choosing to think about what God says.

Now It's Your Turn!

Write 2 Corinthians 10:5 in your own words or copy it out of your favorite Bible translation.

Something to Think About

"You will keep in perfect peace all who trust in You, all whose thoughts are fixed on you!" (Isa. 26:3-4, New Living Translation, NLT)

In My Own Words

Choose your thoughts. Choose your life. I choose to believe what God says.

Something Fun to Do

1. Today, you will need a little bouncy ball. Next, find a spot where it's safe to bounce a ball and start bouncing!
2. Drop it and watch it bounce.
3. See how fast you can pick it up.
4. Count the number of times it bounces before you catch it.
5. Keep practicing until you can catch it in just one bounce!

You can change the game however you want to—you can drop the ball and jump up and down before you catch it or do two jumping jacks really fast and then catch it! But no matter what you do while you're waiting to catch the ball, it will be easier to catch the ball if you keep your eyes on it. As soon as you quit thinking about the ball and start looking at something else, you won't catch it as fast. If you don't believe me, try this and you'll see: First, drop the ball. Second, spin around. Third, grab the ball before it bounces more than once.

That was hard to do, right?

God wants us to keep our eyes on Him the same way that you kept your eyes on the ball. Just like you practiced catching the ball, you can practice focusing on God. Choose your thoughts! God says when we choose to think about Him—how good He is and how much He loves us—we will have peace. Peace is when you feel good. You're not worried or upset. Peace is like your favorite day of the week or a big hug. Peace is when you're happy just being yourself.

Choose Your Thoughts

The next time you start feeling upset about something or worried or scared, just remember to focus on God. He has promised that if we fix our thoughts on Him, He will keep us in perfect peace.

Now It's Your Turn!

Write Isaiah 26:3-4 in your own words or copy it out of your favorite Bible translation.

Lesson 2

How Can I Know God When I Can't Even See Him?

(I'll just tell you now, this story is kind of a longish one, but I promise it's worth it!)

Have you ever wondered how we're supposed to love God and know God when we can't even see God? I have. It's one of my curious questions. I've wondered that pretty much all my life. I've heard about praying to God. I've heard about talking to God. I've heard about listening to God. But I've never seen God.

Mom says that even though we can't see God, we can tell He's there, like the wind when it moves the branches over my tree house. I can't see the wind, but I know it's there because the branches move. Mom says that's how it is with God. She says if I look around me, I will see all kinds of things that show me who God is and tell me what He's like. She says whenever she looks at me, it reminds her of how good God is. Mom says that every time she begins to wonder if God is with her, she just thinks of me and any doubts she has disappear. She says I'm her miracle!

I've been looking for things to show me how good God is and to help me understand Him. The Bible says nature teaches us about God. So I have done some investigating, and I can imagine that God must be very big if He is bigger than the deep blue sky over my head. I also think God must be very funny to create things like doodlebugs. You know those little roly-polies? I decided God must be very loving to give me my family. But that brought up another curious question. What about children who don't have a family? Doesn't God love them? Mom says God loves them every bit as much as He loves me. She says God is always working to help them and protect them, even when they can't see and even when it doesn't look like it from where we are, God is working. Mom says God loves everybody.

I had to ask Mom a few questions about that. How can God love everybody? How can He even *know* everybody?

"Well, to be honest, Emily, there are some things about God I can't explain," Mom admitted. "There are things about God we simply can't understand with our minds. We simply have to believe with our hearts."

"But how can I believe in something I can't see?" I asked. I was sitting on my favorite barstool next to the kitchen window watching the squirrels hop from branch to branch.

"Remember when we talked about the wind blowing the branches of the trees?"

I nodded. "But I want to really see God, Mom!" I pointed at my eyes, "With my eyes! I want to talk to Him and hear Him talk to me." Ugh! Frustrating!

"I know, sweetheart." Mom stopped working on the cinnamon roll dough she was kneading. As she set the rolling pin down, a soft cloud of flour floated up from the counter. She wiped her hands on her apron and came to sit next to me. "It would be nice to talk to God like this, Emily. I agree." She wrapped an arm around my shoulders and kissed my forehead.

I snuggled up next to her. At least I knew for sure that Mom was with me. "I just want to know for sure that God's with me," I said. "For real, like you and Daddy."

Mom looked deep into my green eyes with her brown ones. "Emily, I promise God is with you. He has to be. Without Him, we have no life." She held my face in her hands and kissed my nose. "You'll just have to trust me."

"But, sometimes it feels like I'm just pretending, like I'm just making Him up." I looked at my knees. "Sometimes it seems like the

talks I'm having with God, I'm really just having with me." I felt a little embarrassed.

"Yes, sometimes it feels that way. But, sometimes it doesn't. Sometimes it feels like He's there with you, helping you, right?"

"I guess so." But, I wasn't sure. "How do I know when it's really Him and not just me?"

"Well, first of all, God never tells you anything that isn't in the Bible." Mom got up and pulled her Bible out of the drawer where she keeps it. "The Bible is like a letter that God wrote to you and me. Look at my Bible." She held it up for me. "See how some of the pages are almost falling out?"

"Mm-hmm. It's pretty messy." All kinds of papers and notes were hanging out from between the pages.

"I read my Bible almost every day." Mom set it down on the counter in front of me. "It teaches me. It helps me see God. It helps me hear God when I don't know if I'm hearing God or just hearing me." She pulled out a little pink note that was sticking out between the pages. "This note is from a day when I was thinking about something, and God helped me see the situation differently." The little square of paper had Mom's handwriting all over it in bright red ink. "I keep it in my Bible to remind me of how God helped me and to remember what He said." She picked up the piece of paper and read it. "It's from five years ago."

"That's when I was three," I pointed out. I am really good at figuring out stuff like that.

"That's right! You were three."

"What was the problem God helped you with?" I asked.

"Well, it was the bakery. Back then we didn't live in this house. Remember?" she asked me. "That was before we had the bakery."

"I remember the other house," I said. "Just barely."

"Well, on the day I wrote this note, I was praying." She held it up and looked at it again. "God said not to be afraid, because He was with me. He said that He had everything worked out about the bakery." She dropped the note back between the pages and looked around the room with a happy smile on her face. "I guess He did, didn't He?"

"So what you're saying is that I just have to believe God is with me, even when I can't see Him and even when I'm not sure who's talking, whether it's Him or me?"

"Mm—hmm, that's what I'm saying." Mom washed her hands and then went back to rolling the dough. "The Bible says in Hebrews 11:6 that without faith, it is impossible to please God because anyone who comes to Him must believe that He exists." She looked at me. "That's a bunch of words, isn't it?"

I nodded.

"It just means that we have to believe He's there in order to find Him, and you have to find Him in order to know Him, and you have to know Him in order to love Him …"

"Whoa!" I laughed. "You are talking *too* fast, Mom!"

"Let me give you an example." She closed her eyes to think. (Mom loves to give examples.) "Okay, here's one. If you don't think I'm in the kitchen, will you come looking for me in the kitchen?"

I shook my head.

"Right. Well, God wants you to love Him and to know Him. Before you can love Him and know Him, you have to believe He exists. It's a little bit like this dough." She pointed at the big square of dough with the rolling pin. "If I didn't believe the dough would rise, I wouldn't bother rolling it out into cinnamon rolls. But I *do* believe the dough will rise, so I roll it out to make cinnamon rolls."

"Speaking of the cinnamon rolls, can I help with the cinnamon and sugar?" I asked. That's my favorite part.

"Sure, in just a minute." Mom put brown sugar in a small bowl and set the cinnamon on the counter next to it. "Does all of that make sense, Emily?" she asked me. "That you have to believe God exists in order to love Him?"

"Kind of." I was getting tired of thinking.

"I guess what I'm saying is that faith, or trusting what God says in His Word, even when you can't see it for yourself, is part of the deal. God tells us that. He knows we will struggle because we can't see Him or touch Him."

She pulled an extra barstool around to her side of the counter. "Okay, wash your hands so you can help."

I hopped up from my seat. Putting the cinnamon and brown sugar on the big square of dough is my job! I love the way the cinnamon blends into the golden brown sugar. It's like sand at the beach, but softer. I washed my hands and took my spot at the counter next to Mom.

Mom covered the dough in soft butter, and then she handed the cinnamon and sugar to me. I scooped some brown sugar out of the bowl and spread it over the dough. I love to feel the thick layer of golden brown sugar under my hands as I spread it around. Once the big square of dough is all covered in golden brown sugar, I sprinkle it with cinnamon.

"I think that's one reason God gives us each other," Mom said, still hoping to help me understand. "We learn from our family. Take the cinnamon rolls, for instance. I trust this cinnamon roll recipe will work because your grandmother told me it would. It worked for her. Now, it works for me." Mom added a little more cinnamon to my sugary beach scene and began rolling the dough into a perfect cinnamon and sugared spiral. "When I was first learning, I had to trust what Gramma said, and then finally my own experience proved it to me."

I was beginning to get the picture. "So I can trust God even when I can't see Him because you trust Him and you tell me all about Him?"

"Yes, and you can read about Him in your Bible."

She sliced the spiral of dough into rolls. "Your relationship with God is just between the two of you, Emily.

"God will speak to you in your own heart. I'm only here to help you find your way to Him."

"So you're like the tree branches!" I pointed at Mom. I finally understood! "I know God is here because I see how He lives in you, and that helps me to trust Him."

"I hope so." Mom smiled.

"You're *my* miracle, Mom!" I said, and I leaned over to give her a big kiss. Mom was right. I didn't have to look far to see God. He was right there in the kitchen, making cinnamon rolls with us.

Something to Think About

"Then you will call upon Me and come and pray to Me, and I will listen to you. You will seek Me and find Me when you search for me with all your heart. I will be found by you," declares the Lord. (Jer. 29:12-14 NASB)

In My Own Words

When I pray, God listens. When I look for God, I will find Him. He will make it easy for me to find Him.

Something Fun to Do

Play a quick game of hide-and-seek with someone in your family.

1. The first time you hide, the other person has to look for you. But while he looks for you, he has to be thinking about something else. He can talk on the phone or check his email. He can pass by the TV every few seconds. This time, you stay hidden until he finds you.
2. The second time, you hide again. But while the other person looks for you, he can't do *anything* else. He can't be on the phone or checking the game on TV. He can't be trying to have a conversation with anyone. This time, he is thinking only about finding you. And this time—here's the important part—you have to <u>let</u> him find you! Make it easy! As soon as he starts looking, call out his name so he knows where you might be. You can even jump out to meet him when he gets close!

Sometimes when I pray, I don't feel like God is listening. Sometimes I feel silly talking to God when I can't even see Him or be sure that He's real. But I choose to believe what God says in His Word. He promises that He will let us find Him, and that means He will make it easy!

Choose Your Thoughts

The next time you wonder whether God really hears your prayers or speaks to you in your heart, just remember that He says He will make it easy for us to find Him. If you don't feel like you can really hear God, you can read your Bible out loud or practice saying the memory verse on this page. Worshipping God with a song or a dance helps me feel close to God. Mainly, just don't quit listening for Him! Sometimes my thoughts get so tangled up, it's like being at school and everyone is talking at once. But, even when I can't hear Him or feel Him, His Word says that He's with me. The tree branches blowing in the wind remind me He's there. Look for the things in your world that will remind you that God is with you, and then think about those things!

Now It's Your Turn!

Write Jeremiah 29:12-14 in your own words or copy the verse from your favorite Bible translation.

Something to Think About
Come close to God and God will come close to you. (James 4:8 Amplified Bible, AB)

In My Own Words
When I come close to God, He comes close to me.

Something Fun to Do
Today, you get to make a bookmark for your Bible!

1. Choose two pieces of ribbon.
2. Tie them together at the top with a little knot.
3. Then put something heavy on the knotted end so it won't move, or just hold it between your teeth. (That's what I do!)
4. Wrap the two ribbons around each other until you have one long braid instead of two pieces of ribbon.
5. Tie a knot at the end.

Ta-da! Your bookmark is finished!

As you wrapped the two ribbons around each other, they made one bookmark! Did you know that you can wrap yourself around God? God wants you to have a life that is full of joy and peace and constant closeness to Him. As you think about God and choose His kind of thoughts, you will be more and more aware of His Presence within you. Every time you choose to think God's kind of thoughts, you are wrapping yourself around Him. And as you do, you will live the way He intended you to live—in constant connection to Him!

Choose Your Thoughts
The next time you feel like God isn't with you, start thinking God's kind of thoughts. Wrap yourself around His Word by reading some of the verses from the List of Thoughts Worth Thinking. Wrap yourself around His presence by worshipping with a song or a dance or just by thinking of all of the good things He has done for you.

Choose to think God's kind of thoughts, and pretty soon you will be sure of His presence again.

Now It's Your Turn!

Write James 4:8 in your own words or copy it out of your favorite Bible translation.

Something to Think About

Jesus said, "Anyone who has seen Me, has seen the Father." (John 14:9 AB)

In My Own Words

When I read about Jesus, I learn about God, too, because they are just the same.

Something Fun to Do

1. Pretend that you are a private detective and that you are investigating Jesus. I want you to find out all about Him!
2. Put on a costume and dress up like a detective.
3. Find out all kinds of things that Jesus did. How did He act? What did He say? How did He treat other people? What did He tell people about God? What did He teach people? Do you know where to look? I looked in my Bible. Here are some verses that tell us about Jesus: John 15:15, Matthew 9:11-13, Matthew 16:30-38, Matthew 20:29-34, Matthew 22:36-40, John 12:44-50, Mark 10:45, Luke 6:27-38, Luke 7:36-50, Colossians 1:15. See if you can find more!
4. Write down a description of Jesus that would help someone who did not know Him to know who He was and what He did.
5. Draw a picture of Jesus. He can be doing something that you discovered He did, or it can just be a picture of Him looking at you. However you see Jesus, use your colored pencils to draw Him on a piece of paper.

Sometimes it's hard to trust God when you can't see Him. But Jesus said that if we have seen Him, then we have seen the Father. So you can be sure that God is just like Jesus. He cared when people were sad and hurting. He forgave people for their sins. He helped people learn how to have a relationship with God. What else did you discover about Jesus?

Choose Your Thoughts

The next time you wonder what God is like, read about Jesus in your Bible. Any time you begin to wonder if God really loves you or wants to help you solve problems or answer your questions, read about Jesus. When you read about Jesus, you will see that God wants you to love Him and to know that He loves you.

Now It's Your Turn!

Write John 14:9 using your own words or copy it out of your favorite Bible translation.

Lesson 3

How Do I Know God Loves Me?

(This is a super important curious question! You don't want to miss this!)

How do I know God loves me?

Maybe that's one of your questions, too. It was one of mine. It's one of the very first questions you have to ask when you are learning to think.

Let's say you are just going along one day, having fun with your friends. Maybe you're at school, or maybe you're playing outside at someone's house. Everything is great! You know what I mean? And then something happens, something not so great. Something that is, in fact, a teensy, tiny bit irritating. Maybe it's something like your best friend says you're bossy or your best friend starts *being* bossy. Suddenly, you go from having so much fun to having no fun at all. Your feelings are hurt, and you're so mad that you have to go home!

That's when you know it's time to choose your thoughts.

Don't worry. You'll know when the time comes. It's easy because it's basically any time you have a problem. As soon as I think I have a problem or a question that I just don't know the answer to, the first thing I always do is ask myself this question: "Does God love me?" I know the answer is yes. But sometimes I need to think it through, and that brings us back to our question for today: how do I know God loves me?

Well, for starters, as soon as I ask, God tells me He loves me. It's kind of like an echo. Have you ever heard an echo? It's kind of like that. One time, He answered before I even finished asking, "God, do you love me?" Before I said two words, I heard His answer in my heart: "Yes, Emily," He said. "I love you. I've always loved you, and I will never stop loving you. My love for you is bigger than the sky over your head, and just like the sky covers you and is with you everywhere you go, I am with you and my love is with you, everywhere you go."

Sometimes God doesn't even say anything; I just know. One time when I was feeling sad, a butterfly landed next to me. It opened its little wings, and I saw beautiful flashes of blue and black. I felt so happy inside! I knew it was just a little reminder from God that He loves me.

God's Word tells me He loves me. There are so many verses in the Bible where God tells us and shows us that He loves us. Several of the verses are in this book! Because like I said, knowing God loves you is the first step in learning how to think!

So let's review and see if you got it. How do you know God loves you? He tells you as soon as you ask. Before you even get the question out, you will know in your heart, deep down inside, that God loves you. And even if you're not sure about that, His Word tells you He loves you. And hey! *I'm* telling you—God loves you!

Now, it's your turn. Go ahead—ask God if He loves you. I bet you'll hear the answer before you even finish the question, just like an echo. God will tell you He loves you. Go on. Ask Him. You'll see!

Something to Think About

For I am convinced that neither death, nor life, nor angels, nor principalities, nor things present, nor things to come, nor powers, nor height, nor depth, nor any other created thing will be able to separate us from the love of God, which is in Christ Jesus our Lord. (Rom. 8:38-39 NASB)

In My Own Words

Nothing, absolutely nothing, is ever going to take God's love away from me. Nothing. No way. No how.

Something Fun to Do

Spread your arms as far apart as you can. As far away as they might be, they are still connected to your body. See what I mean?

It's the same with God's love. Nothing can separate you from the love of God. No matter what you do or how far away you try to go, God will not stop loving you. No matter how you look or how you feel, you cannot lose God's love. Even if you don't love God, He still loves you. Even if you get mad at God, He still loves you. Nothing you do or anyone else does will ever change God's love for you. God loves you, no matter what—forever.

Choose Your Thoughts

The next time you wonder whether or not God loves you, stretch your arms as wide apart as they will go and remember that nothing can separate you from God's love.

Now It's Your Turn!

Write Romans 8:38 in your own words or copy it out of your favorite Bible translation.

Something to Think About
May you experience the love of Christ, though it is too great to understand fully. (Eph. 3:19 NLT)

In My Own Words
I don't have to understand God's love to feel it.

Something Fun to Do
Today you are going to experience something. Do you know what that means? It is sort of like getting to know a place. You learn about a place by being there. You learn about how food tastes by tasting it. When you taste a food, you experience the food. And today, that is what I want you to do!

1. Pick out one of your favorite foods and take a few bites.
2. Does it taste as good as you thought it would?
3. While you eat your favorite food, think about it. Why do you like it? When is your favorite time to eat it? Is it sweet or sour? Is it crunchy? Is it chewy?

As you thought about all of those questions, you were experiencing your favorite food. You were noticing things about it. Do you understand why your favorite food tastes the way it does? You might understand a little bit, but probably not all of the details, right? Well, here's some good news—you don't have to understand why it tastes good to know that it tastes good! And we don't have to understand how God loves us or why He loves us to know that He loves us. Right there in Ephesians 3:19, God tells us that His love is so great that we can't understand it.

But we can experience it! When you experience something, it becomes real to you. It's like snow. You can know in your head that snow is cold, but until you put your hand in it, you don't really know what cold snow feels like. God wants you to feel His love in your heart. The Bible tells us in Romans 5:5 NLT, "He has given us the Holy Spirit to fill our hearts with His love." You don't have to do anything. The Holy Spirit has already filled your heart with God's love. One of the easiest ways to experience God's love is to love someone else. When we love others, we are experiencing God. That is why the Bible says in 1 John 4:16 AB, "God is love, and he who dwells and continues in love dwells and continues in God and God dwells and continues in him."

Choose Your Thoughts

The next time you wonder whether God really loves you, find a way to experience His love. You can think of how good God has been to you. You can show love to someone else. Don't try to understand it; just experience it!

Now It's Your Turn!

Write Ephesians 3:19 in your own words, or copy it out of your favorite Bible translation.

Something to Think About
See how very much our Father loves us, for he calls us his children, and that is what we are! (1 John 3:1 NLT)

In My Own Words
God loves me so much that He calls me His child!

Something Fun to Do
What does the word *family* mean to you? What do you think it means to be someone's child? How does that feel? When God calls us His children, it means that He treasures us very much. Have you ever played house? Or family?

When I play house, I pretend to be the mother of my parakeet, Buddy. I love Buddy. He is very small with bright green and yellow feathers. He has a beautiful blue dot on each side of his head. Sometimes when I hold him, he pecks at me with his little beak. It doesn't hurt. Well, one time it did. Anyway, I pretend to be the mama bird and Buddy is my baby. I feed him and give him water. I protect him from the ceiling fan by turning it off whenever he flies around. I clean his cage. And, of course, I make sure he has fun little toys to play with and his beak scratcher.

Today, here's what I want you to do:

1. Pretend you're a parent.
2. What would you name your child?
3. What kinds of fun things would you do with your child?
4. How would you show your child that you loved him or her?

I'll bet you wanted your child to feel loved right? Well, that's just how God feels about you! He treasures you. You are His child. He wants to take good care of you and make sure that you have everything you need! He wants you to know that you're loved! That's why He sent Jesus to be our Savior, so that we could know God's love.

Choose Your Thoughts

The next time you wonder if God loves you, remember that He calls you His child. He has made you a member of His family. He loves you and wants to take care of you. Remember how much your child mattered to you when you were pretending? You matter even more to God. His love for you is always there.

Now It's Your Turn!

Write 1 John 3:1 in your own words or copy it out of your favorite Bible translation.

Lesson 4

Seeing Yourself the Way God Sees You

One day at lunch, I was carrying my tray to the table. I don't know what happened, but it started to slip. The bowl of applesauce slid right off and fell with a big splat all over my new shoes—my *favorite* new shoes! Anyway, now they are covered in sticky applesauce. Can you say *embarrassing*? Everyone turned around and looked at me because the bowl crashed *really loud* when it hit the floor. Silverware went flying everywhere! I'm pretty sure my whole face turned red. The lunch lady was *not* happy. She huffed and puffed and rolled her eyes at me when she saw what had happened, and then she pushed the big mop pail over and started cleaning it up. I told her I was sorry. She just looked at the ground and shook her head. "Be more careful, please," she said, not very nicely.

Everyone was laughing at me when I got to the table, everyone but Grace. "Way to go!" Christopher said, and he pretended to be me, dropping my tray. "Whoa! I think it's gonna fall!" he snickered.

"Everyone leave Emily alone!" Grace yelled. "You are making her feel bad!"

I just looked at my plate and tried not to notice the applesauce squishing through the tops of my shoes. Usually, only the little kids drop their food. I am not a little kid. I'm eight. The kindergarteners and first graders had all stared at me like they couldn't believe it. I wanted to go home.

When we finally left the lunchroom, my shoes were sticking to

the floor and made little crackling, squeaking sounds with every step. *Great*, I thought, *my brand new shoes are ruined!*

"Emily, why don't you go and wipe off the bottom of your shoes with a wet paper towel," suggested Ms. Michaels. "The janitor doesn't want you tracking footprints everywhere." Ugh. So embarrassing.

I walked straight to the bathroom. After I cleaned off the bottoms of my shoes, I tried to clean off the tops. I ran water over them in the sink. Unfortunately, all that did was make my shoes really, really wet, and they still smelled like applesauce! *Guh-ross*. I never knew one little bowl could hold so much.

When I got back to class, I asked Ms. Michaels if I could call my mother. I told her I wanted to go home.

"There is no reason to call home for applesauce on your shoes. You'll be okay, Emily," was all she said.

My shoes made squishing noises all the way back to my desk. I could feel the water soaking into my socks.

The rest of the day took forever. My shoes and socks never dried. Every time I thought about spilling my tray, I just felt more embarrassed. "You couldn't help it, Emily," Grace said while we were doing partner work. "It was an accident."

"I know, but it's still embarrassing. And I keep thinking about how everyone was laughing at me," I told her. I wiggled my toes in my wet shoes. "And these shoes feel disgusting."

When it was finally time to go home, I climbed into the car and took my shoes and socks off right away.

"How was your day?" Mom asked from the front.

"Embarrassing," I told her.

She turned to look at me over her shoulder. "Embarrassing? What happened?"

"Well, I was walking from the food line to the table, and my tray slipped. And I spilled applesauce all over my new shoes," I blurted.

"Oh no," Mom said. "I'm sorry, Emily. I bet you did feel a little embarrassed, didn't you?"

"Not just a little. A lot." I frowned. "Everybody was laughing at me."

"Well, you didn't do it on purpose," she pointed out. "And they shouldn't have laughed. I'm sorry that happened." She reached back to pat my leg. "I'm sorry, sweetheart."

"I wanted to call you so I could come home, but Ms. Michaels said no."

"Well, that was a good decision. You made it just fine through the rest of the day. We have to save those phone calls for when you're sick and need to come home and rest."

"Well, I really needed to come home today. I was embarrassed and my shoes were soaking wet!" *How could she not understand this?*

"How much applesauce did you get?" Mom asked. "It couldn't have gotten your shoes that wet."

"I tried to rinse them off in the sink," I explained.

"Oh, Emily." Mom laughed. "Poor thing."

I didn't laugh with her. The kids at school had all laughed at me, and now she was laughing at me, too. I just glared out the window.

"I'm sorry you had a bad day, Emily," Mom said softly after a few seconds.

I didn't answer her. Now, I was embarrassed *and* mad! I watched the cars driving next to us and tried to count the trees as we passed them on the street. I didn't want to cry—that would just be more embarrassing!

"Emily?" Mom waited for me to answer.

"Yes, ma'am?" I said quietly.

"I'm sorry. I didn't mean to hurt your feelings."

"You laughed at me!" I stared harder out the window at the street. We were pulling into our driveway.

"I'm sorry."

"Everyone at school laughed at me!" I yelled. "I don't like for people to laugh at me. It's embarrassing. I think I might be embarrassed forever!"

"Only if you choose to be." Mom turned to look at me before she got out of the car. "Whaddya think?" She smiled. "Is that what you choose? To be embarrassed forever?"

"No." I shook my head.

"Good." Mom stepped out of the car. "Being embarrassed forever is boring."

"Okay, okay. I know it's time to choose my thoughts." I knew what she was about to say and I did *not* want to hear it.

As soon as I put away my backpack, I went straight out to my tree house. If I didn't want to be embarrassed forever, I was going to have to choose my thoughts. I grabbed my Bible and my List of Thoughts Worth Thinking. They were under my enormous pile of dress-ups, as usual.

It was time to practice thinking! I asked myself the very first, most important, question: "Does God love me?" I always ask this question first when I am choosing my thoughts, and then I wiggle my toes and squeeze my eyes shut tight. I know God loves me. God tells me He loves me every time I ask Him. His Word tells me He loves me. And all of the good things in my life remind me that God loves me. Yes! God loves me!

I asked myself the second question: "What does God say about me?" I looked at my List of Thoughts Worth Thinking.

"Thought 1: God says He made me just the way He wants me, and He is proud of me, just the way I am."

Everyone else might be making fun of me, but God says He loves me and He is proud of me, no matter what.

I had to make a decision.

(This is where learning to think really changes things! This is where you have to choose your thoughts.)

This is what I do every time I am getting ready to think.

I say to myself, *Emily, prepare to think.* I close my eyes and wiggle my toes. I think. It's pretty simple, really. I can choose to think about what God says, or I can think about what people say.

When I thought about what the kids at school said, I felt embarrassed and bad about myself. But when I thought about what God says, I felt good. I felt loved.

So I had to decide. I had to choose my thoughts.

I closed my eyes and wiggled my toes again. I said to myself, *Emily, prepare to think!* Then, I imagined myself the way God sees me—loved, special, perfectly me, Emily. I realized that it really didn't matter what the kids at school said; they would forget about it next week. And who cares if I spilled applesauce on my shoes? That didn't change who I am! I'm the person God made me. I'm perfectly me, Emily!

What about you? Do you have a story about a time when you felt embarrassed? What did you choose to think about?

Something to Think About

For God made Christ, who never sinned, to be the offering for our sin, so that we could be made right with God through Christ. (2 Cor. 5:21 NLT)

In My Own Words

Jesus took my place.

Something Fun to Do

1. Ask an adult to help you with this activity.
2. You need a clean piece of cloth or a paper towel and some furniture polish.
3. Now, it's time to find some dust! I like to wait until the sun shines through the windows. I look around at all of the tables until I find one that has little tiny dust particles floating all around it. Usually, that will be a great place to do this activity! If you have any furniture in your room, like a dresser, it will work too.
4. Take your clean cloth. Look at it very closely. See how clean it is?
5. Now add some furniture polish.
6. And here's the fun part—polish that table until it shines!
7. How does it look?
8. Now look at your cloth. How does it look? Dirty, right?

Think of yourself as the table and the cloth as Jesus. The dust is like your sin. Sin keeps us from shining like we should. But Jesus traded places with us. He took the sin that separated us from God. When you ask Jesus to live in your heart and forgive you for your sins, God wipes away all of the dust (sin) from your life. You never have to feel separated from God again. All you have to do is shine!

Choose Your Thoughts

The next time you feel like you've made too many mistakes for God to love you, stop and remember—God sees you through Jesus.

Because of Jesus, God only sees the good in you. Because Jesus took your sin, nothing can ever separate you from God. Choose to see yourself the way God sees you—whole and complete. You are just the way you are supposed to be—ready to shine!

Now It's Your Turn!

Write 2 Corinthians 5:21 in your own words or copy it out of your favorite Bible translation.

Something to Think About

God has united you with Christ Jesus. For our benefit God made Him to be wisdom itself. Christ made us right with God; He made us pure and holy, and he freed us from sin. (1 Cor. 1:30 NLT)

In My Own Words

God made me just the way He wants me in Jesus.

Something Fun to Do

You will need some scissors, a magazine, a glue stick, and a clean piece of paper.

1. Cut out a picture of a person from a magazine. (Try to get a picture that has the whole person showing, from the head to the toes.)
2. Now, carefully cut your picture up into a few pieces like you are going to make it into a puzzle.
3. Rearrange the picture so that it doesn't look right. You can put things where they don't belong, like a foot where the hand should be or maybe the face on the person's stomach. It looks pretty silly, doesn't it?
4. Now take it apart and put it all back together the right way.
5. Use your glue stick to glue it all in place on your clean piece of paper.
6. Perfect, right?

Righteousness is God's way of doing and being right. Without righteousness, we are like the picture with all the pieces in the wrong place. The only way we can be righteous is by having God live inside of us. Being righteous means living in perfect harmony with God. Jesus gave us His righteousness when He died on the cross and took our sins. Our sins are all those things we do to try and make ourselves look right, feel right, and be right, but they never work! Through Jesus's death on the cross and His resurrection, God has made you whole, just the way He intended for you to be! He has put you in a perfect relationship with Him. Just like you fixed the picture back to its original form, when God made you righteous in Jesus, He put all of your pieces back exactly the way He wanted them.

Choose Your Thoughts

The next time you feel like you're all wrong, like you're just one big mistake, remind yourself that God has made you righteous. Jesus took your sin and gave you His perfect relationship with God. You never have to worry about being accepted. Jesus accepts you and loves you, and He has made you whole and complete, perfect in Him.

Now It's Your Turn!

Write 1 Corinthians 1:30 in your own words or copy it out of your favorite Bible translation.

Note from Emily

Hi, it's me, Emily! How do you like the book so far? Are you learning anything new about your thoughts? Have you gotten a few chances to practice thinking? I hope so!

I decided that you might need a few new thoughts to get started. Sometimes when I am thinking about something and I know I need to think about it differently, I need a new thought to think. Know what I mean?

So, here it is. It's my very own list that I'm gonna share with you!

A List of Thoughts Worth Thinking

#1 GOD MADE ME JUST THE WAY I AM AND HE IS PROUD OF ME

2 CORINTHIANS 8:7 CHRIST HAD NO SIN, BUT GOD MADE HIM BECOME SIN, SO IN CHRIST WE COULD BECOME RIGHT WITH GOD.

#2 GOD LOVES ME FOREVER, NO MATTER WHAT.

1 JOHN 3:1 WHAT AN INCREDIBLE QUALITY OF LOVE THE FATHER HAS GIVEN US THAT WE SHOULD BE CALLED CHILDREN OF GOD.

EPHESIANS 3:19 MAY YOU

A List of Thoughts Worth Thinking

Thought #1:
God made me just the way I am and He is proud of me.

2 Corinthians 5:21 NLT—For God made Christ, who never sinned, to be the offering for our sin, so that we could be made right with God through Christ.

1 Corinthians 1:30 NLT—God has united you with Christ Jesus. For our benefit God made Him to be wisdom itself. Christ made us right with God; He made us pure and holy, and He freed us from sin.

Thought #2:
God loves me, forever, no matter what.

1 John 3:1 NLT—See how very much our Father loves us, for he calls us his children, and that is what we are!

Ephesians 3:19 NLT—May you experience the love of Christ, though it is too great to understand fully.

Romans 8:38-39 NASB—For I am convinced that neither death, nor life, nor angels, nor principalities, nor things present, nor things to come, nor powers, nor height, nor depth, nor any other created thing will be able to separate us from the love of God, which is in Christ Jesus our Lord.

Thought #3:
God is always with me.

Jeremiah 29:12-14 NASB—"Then you will call upon Me and come and pray to Me, and I will listen to you. You will seek Me and find Me when you search for me with all your heart. I will be found by you," declares the Lord.

John 16:32 AB—Yet I am not alone, because the Father is with me.

Psalm 95:2 AB—Let us come to Him with thanksgiving.

Joshua 1:9 AB—Be not afraid, neither be dismayed for the Lord your God is with you, wherever you go.

Thought #4:
God has good plans for me.

John 16:13 AB—But when He, the Spirit of Truth (the Truth-giving Spirit) comes, He will guide you into all the Truth.

Proverbs 3:5-6 NASB—Trust in the Lord with all of your heart, lean not on your own understanding. In all of your ways, acknowledge Him and He will keep your paths straight.

Jeremiah 29:11 NLT—"For I know the plans I have for you," says the Lord. "They are plans for good and not for disaster, to give you a future and a hope."

Thought #5:
God has forgiven me and made me new in Jesus.

Philippians 3:13 NLT—Forgetting the past and looking forward to what lies ahead, I press on to reach the end of the race and receive the heavenly prize for which God, through Christ Jesus, is calling us.

Hebrews 10:17 NASB—Their sins I will remember no more.

Thought #6:
I can do anything God calls me to do because He will help me.

Ephesians 3:16 AB—May He grant you out of the rich treasury of His glory, to be strengthened and reinforced with mighty power in the inner man, by the Holy Spirit Himself indwelling your innermost being and personality.

Psalm 31:24 NASB—Be strong and let your heart take courage, all you who hope in the Lord.

Psalm 71:5 AB—For You are my hope; O Lord God, You are my trust from my youth and the source of my confidence.

Thought #7:
I can choose my thoughts, and that means I can choose my life.

Isaiah 26:3-4 NLT—You will keep in perfect peace all who trust in You, all whose thoughts are fixed on You!

2 Corinthians 10:5 NASB—We are taking every thought captive to the obedience of Christ.

Thought #8:
God listens to me.

James 5:16 NIV—The prayer of a righteous person is powerful and effective.

Jeremiah 29:12-14 NASB—"Then you will call upon Me and come and pray to Me, and I will listen to you. You will seek Me and find Me when you search for me with all your heart. I will be found by you," declares the Lord.

Thought #9:
God understands me.

Hebrews 4:15 NLT—This High Priest of ours understands our weaknesses, for He faced all of the same testings we do, yet He did not sin.

Psalm 139:1-3, 14 NIV—You have searched me, Lord, and you know me.... You are familiar with all my ways.... I praise you because I am fearfully and wonderfully made.

Lesson 5

When Choosing Your Thoughts Is *Not* the Best Choice

You don't want to skip this one! It may look a little longer than the others, but that's because there is some extremely critical you-just-gotta-know info! So read on, and prepare to think!

This lesson is all about your feelings. Don't let anyone tell you your feelings are not important! Never, ever, no matter what, believe that your feelings aren't important. Your feelings are *your* feelings—nobody else's—and they are real! Your feelings tell you all kinds of things about yourself. You must absolutely listen to them!

Got it? Good!

For example, being afraid is one of the worst feelings in the world. I hate being afraid. Sometimes the things we are afraid of aren't even real, like a scary dream. You wake up, and you know it wasn't real. But you still feel a little scared.

Unfortunately, sometimes the things we are afraid of *are* real. And the worst part is, sometimes they don't go away. Sometimes just choosing different thoughts will not solve your problem. When you have one of those times, don't stay all by yourself and try to choose your thoughts. Go to your mom or dad or another grown-up who loves you and tell them how you feel.

Your feelings are like the gauge in your car that tells when the gas tank is empty. If your car is about to run out of gas, you aren't going to fill it back up by choosing your thoughts! The same is true for you. If your heart is hurting, if you are really sad or scared about something, find someone to talk to! Let someone know how you are feeling. Friends are great people to share your feelings with, but sometimes friends might not be quite as helpful as grown-ups. Believe it or not, grown-ups *do* understand us sometimes! I hope you have a grown-up in your life you can trust. A grown-up you can trust will make you feel safe and comfortable. They will listen to you.

Now, just to be sure you've got it—it is always good to share your feelings with someone else, but there are some times when it is *super-duper important*! I have listed a few of those times here:

1. If someone is hurting you
2. If someone is hurting someone you love
3. If someone makes you feel uncomfortable or yucky inside
4. If someone makes you feel bad about yourself
5. If someone wants you to do something but doesn't want you to tell anyone else about it
6. If you feel really sad and the feeling never goes away
7. If you feel really lonely
8. If you feel like no one cares about you

If you are in one of those situations, please go to a grown-up you trust and tell them how you feel. That's what I do. If the first person doesn't help you, then just keep asking for help until someone does.

And of course, it's always important to talk to God. He is always listening to us, and He has promised to help us. But like I said, not every scary or sad situation will go away. At those times, it is really important for you to know that God gives us His Holy Spirit to be our comforter. He can comfort you when you are sad or worried or afraid. That's when you can practice choosing your thoughts, not to make your feelings go away but to feel God's love for you right in the middle of your feelings! It's sort of like a flashlight in the dark; right there in the middle of all that darkness, turn on your flashlight and, ta-da! There's light! (Check out the activities after Lesson 7 for this very experiment!)

Now, let's go back to my example of being afraid. One time, I had to choose my thoughts right in the middle of being afraid. In my case, I wasn't in any real danger. I knew I was safe. My parents and I had been climbing a ropes course all day. My dad kept calling it our "family adventure." We were up high in the trees climbing around on skinny little cables and jumping from spot to spot. We were all hooked in with a harness and ropes, and guides were there to help us. I knew we were safe. But every time I looked down, I would think about how terrible it would be to fall to the bottom. I don't know why I kept thinking about that! I just did. Anyway, it took me a little while, but finally I learned to look straight ahead at where I was going instead of looking at the ground below me. Everything was much better after that, until we got to the end. At the very end, there was a big jump called the Leap of Faith. You had to stand on the edge of a teeny, tiny platform, jump out into the air, and catch a trapeze that was extremely far away!

"No way." I shook my head when we got to the last platform and I saw the trapeze dangling in the distance. "That is too far away."

I looked from the edge of the platform to the trapeze. I pictured myself trying to reach for it and missing. "What happens if you miss?" I asked the guide. He looked relaxed and happy. He had a big smile on his face.

"Oh, no problem! You just fall into the net." The guide shrugged and nodded his head toward the ground.

"Where is the net?" I asked.

"Right beneath us," he said.

I looked down and saw the net. "That is a long way down." I really did not want to do this. "Is there another way?"

"Sure," he said. "You can take the slide." He pointed to a slide that was a few feet away.

"Emily, you don't want to miss out on the Leap of Faith!" Dad said. "You can't leave without trying. You'll love it!"

"I don't know, Dad." I shook my head and looked at the trapeze again. "I might hate it."

"What you'll really hate is going home, knowing you didn't even try," Dad argued.

"Maybe," I said. "But I don't want to fall all the way to that net."

"You're still hooked in," Dad pointed out. "It's not a free fall."

"Yeah, but it scares me."

"What about you, Honey?" Dad asked Mom. "Are you ready to take the Leap of Faith?"

Mom looked at me. "I will if Emily will." *Oh great*, I thought, *now if I don't go, Mom will miss out.*

"Ugh. Mom, that is *not* fair!" I told her. "I'm too scared."

"Well, I'm going!" Dad said happily. I could tell he had been waiting for this moment all day. "See you two at the bottom, however you get there!"

I knew it was time to make a decision. I had to choose my thoughts, but I was really scared. I might miss the trapeze and fall all the way to the net! They said it wouldn't be too bad, but it was a long way to fall. I closed my eyes and wiggled my toes in my shoes.

I asked myself the first question: "Does God love me?"

I thought about how God showed me He loved me all the time. Just that afternoon, I'd found a butterfly's wing. It was buried in the pine needles on one of the paths. The bright color stood out against the dull, brown needles covering the ground. I was sad that the butterfly must have died, but I was amazed at the beautiful silvery spots on the bright orange wing. I picked it up carefully. It was so delicate. It didn't even look real!

Dad was getting ready to take off. I had to make a decision. I took the fragile wing out of my pocket. It was wrapped in a tissue for safekeeping. I turned to protect my treasure from the breeze and looked at the fragile little wing. Its tiny details were shining in the sunlight like a painting in a museum.

"What do you think, Emily?" Mom asked me.

"I know God is with me," I said. "And I know He loves me and His Word tells me that I don't have to be afraid."

"That's true." Dad nodded.

"But I'm still afraid," I said.

"That's okay," Mom said. "We all get scared sometimes. You make the choice that feels right for you."

I closed my eyes super tight. I wiggled my toes. *God cherishes me more than I cherish this little wing*, I thought.

"Okay," I said. I had made my decision.

I tucked the wing back into its bed of tissue and put it safely in my pocket.

"I'll do it!"

The guide nodded and patted me on the back. "Good choice!" He said. "You'll love it. Even if you fall, it's fun to land! Trust me—I've done it tons of times!"

"You have?" I asked.

"Yeah, they make us do all kinds of stuff when we're getting ready for this job." He smiled and hooked me up to a new set of ropes.

No wonder he's so relaxed, I thought. *He already knows how it feels to fall. He already knows the net will catch him.*

I stepped out to the edge of the platform. I thought of all of the times God had been there for me. I thought of the little wing in my pocket that was so amazing that I knew only God could have created it. I felt all tingly in my feet, and my stomach was flipping like crazy. I looked straight ahead at the trapeze. I kept my eyes focused on where I wanted to go. I still felt scared, but I knew God was with me. I shut my eyes and jumped! I reached out for the trapeze, and guess what! I caught it! I couldn't believe it! I hadn't even opened my eyes, and I still caught it!

That was a great day! God helped me by reminding me that He loved me. His Holy Spirit comforted me. I felt safe inside because I knew God was with me. And I had my parents with me to encourage me and tell me I was safe.

Talking to God is a great way to hear His voice. Reading your Bible and looking at the List of Thoughts Worth Thinking are super ways to choose God's kind of thoughts. But choosing God's kind of thoughts is never going to stop us from needing other people. God made us to need Him and to need one another. I mean, how fun would it be to tell the funniest joke ever if no one was there to laugh with you?

So just remember—listen to your feelings. They matter. Talk to someone when you feel sad or scared or lonely. You can't solve every problem by choosing your thoughts, but as long as you keep choosing God's kind of thoughts, He will lead you through whatever problems you might face.

Something to Think About

Be not afraid, neither be dismayed, for the Lord your God is with you, wherever you go. (Josh. 1:9 AB)

In My Own Words

God is with me, and I can trust Him.

Something Fun to Do

Today I want you to get out your crayons or colored pencils and some paper!

1. Draw a picture of you and God walking together. Remember, it doesn't have to be perfect. It doesn't even have to look like two people—just whatever you see in your imagination, okay?
2. Then, draw a big circle around you and God.
3. Color the area outside of the circle a color that you think looks scary.
4. Color the area inside the circle a nice, clear, happy color. It will be a background for you and God.

That's it! Easy one, huh?

God doesn't promise us that scary or sad things won't happen, but He does promise us that He will be with us at all times. The situations around you might not change, but God will be with you. A few stories in the Bible describe what it's like to trust God while you go through a hard situation. One of my favorite stories is the story of Joseph. You can read all about Joseph in the book of Genesis. Joseph's brothers sold him into slavery. That was terrible! It wasn't Joseph's fault, and he couldn't do anything about it. But God was with Joseph, and Joseph kept on trusting God. Then Joseph ended up in jail, and again, it was not his fault And again, it was terrible and he couldn't do anything about it. But he still trusted God. Joseph still honored God, even when things were pretty bad. He never doubted that God loved him. (I think that's why he kept on trusting God. I mean, it's pretty hard to trust someone who you think is going to hurt you, right?) In the end, Joseph became the second-most important man in Egypt! Everything worked out for Joseph just like God told him it would in the beginning. It is a great story, even though there were some really sad and really scary parts. Check it out for yourself in Genesis 36, 37, 39, and 40-45. (It's kind of a long story, but it has a *great* ending!)

Choose Your Thoughts

The next time you are facing a scary or a sad situation, choose to think about God's promise—He is always with you. Trust Him to comfort you and guide you. The situation may or may not change, but your heart, the deepest part of you, will be safe with God. Remember, you should always listen to your feelings! If you skipped the story for this lesson, go back and read it. There are some times when choosing your thoughts is *not* the best choice!

Now It's Your Turn!

Write Joshua 1:9 in your own words or copy it out of your favorite Bible translation.

Something to Think About

And we know that God causes everything to work together for good to those who love God, to those who are called according to His purpose. (Rom. 8:28 NASB)

In My Own Words

I can trust God to work everything out for me, even my problems, because I love Him. I know He has a good purpose for me.

Something Fun to Do

Do you know how to make a thumbprint? Today, your art will begin with a thumbprint. Here's how you do it!

1. Color the tip of your thumb, the part you can press onto paper, with a marker. Get plenty of ink on your thumb.
2. Now, press your inky thumb onto your paper. Make a nice thumbprint.
3. Once you make your thumbprint, take your markers and create a "doodle bug." You can use swirly lines, straight lines, thin or thick lines, short lines or long lines. Keep doodling on and around your thumbprint until you have a bug.
4. Name your bug!

Wasn't that fun? You created a piece of art from your thumbprint! No one else will have a bug just like yours! God does the same thing with our mistakes and problems. God is so full of love for us that even when something bad happens or we mess up, God works it all out so that in the end, it helps us and doesn't hurt us. That doesn't mean that God makes bad things happen to us. God is good and only good. We are in a perfect relationship with Him through Jesus, so we know that because of Jesus, God is not mad at us!

But sometimes our mistakes get in the way and we take a different path than the one God intended. Sometimes, someone *else* does the wrong thing and *their* mistake gets in the way, forcing us to take a detour. But not for long! God is like the superhero who never quits and never fails! He will find you on whatever path you're on, and He will, one way or another, get you right back where He wanted you to go in the first place. He's just that good. He's so awesome! He doesn't even need a cape! Oh, and don't forget, if you haven't read it yet, check out the story of Joseph—Genesis 36, 37, 39, 40-45.

Choose Your Thoughts

The next time you feel like everything in your life is going wrong or like your situation is hopeless, make a doodle bug! Remind yourself that God sees your situation and He is going to work it out for your good.

Now It's Your Turn!

Write Romans 8:28 in your own words or copy it out of your favorite Bible translation.

Lesson 6

What to Do When You Feel Lonely

(Curious question from a not-so-great day in my life. This one is directly from my personal diary.)

Ugh. I feel lonely.

It hasn't been a very good day. Grace was absent, and I didn't have anyone to be my partner for partner work. I also didn't have anyone to sit with at lunch. It was *not* a very good day.

Since we got home, Mom has been really busy with work. Roxy is at the kennel getting a bath, so she isn't home today.

I finished all my homework, so I went to see if someone can play. I went to Grace's house, but nobody was there. I went to Katie's house, but she was at dance. I tried Brooke's house, but her brother said she had gone to the horse barn.

When I got back home, Mom was still busy taking orders over the phone. She waved at me and blew me a little kiss. I blew her a kiss back and went out to sit down on the back steps. I thought about playing in my tree house, but I am tired of playing imaginary games all by myself. I want a friend to play with me—a real person! I know God is with me, but I can't really see Him.

Then, the sun started getting really hot on my head, so I got up and headed over to the tree house anyway. I climbed the ladder. It goes red step, yellow step, purple step, blue step, yellow step, red step, and finally purple step. I pushed open the little wooden door, and a fly buzzed past me—not quite who I had in mind for company.

Once I was inside, I lay down on my back in the middle of the floor and stared up at the tree branches through the roof. I could see the sky peeking through the bright green leaves. They're beginning to turn orange. I felt so lonely. It kind of felt like no one cares about me. I figured I needed to choose my thoughts. My thoughts can change my feelings. I wiggled my toes and squeezed my eyes shut. I had to make a decision. How did I want to feel?

Well, for sure, I was tired of feeling lonely. So, I got up and got my Thinking Book from underneath my big pile of dress-ups in the corner. I opened it to the first page, which says, "Choose your thoughts. Choose your life." I turned the page and saw, "Does God love me?" That is always the first question I ask when I am choosing my thoughts. I stopped. I wiggled my toes and squeezed my eyes shut tight. I told myself, "Emily, prepare to think." And then I thought. *Does God love me?* The Bible tells me that God is love and that nothing can ever separate me from God's love. I thought about all of the good things in my life. God must love me to be so good to me. *Yep, I'm sure God loves me.*

"Thank you, God, for loving me," I said out loud. I am so thankful that the God who created the whole world loves me. "I love you," I told Him.

I turned the page. "What does God say about me?" I stopped, wiggled my toes, and squeezed my eyes shut. I thought. God says so many things about me that I can't remember them all, so I turned to the List of Thoughts Worth Thinking. I ran my finger down the list and stopped at, "God says I am never alone."

Hmmm, looks like I have to make a decision, I thought. *Am I going to think my own thoughts, or will I choose to believe God and think like He does?*

I turned the page: "What do I choose to think about?" I squeezed my eyes shut. I wiggled my toes. God says I am not alone. Could that be true? Deep down inside, I know it is. I know God loves me, and I know He tells the truth.

If that's true, I don't have to feel lonely, even when I am alone. I closed my eyes and wiggled my toes. He loves me, and He will never leave me. I choose to believe what God says. He loves me. He will never leave me. Now, instead of feeling lonely, I choose to think about what God says. I feel happy because I know God loves me and will never leave me.

Now it's your turn. Have you ever had a day when you felt lonely? What did you choose to think about?

Something to Think About

Let us come before His Presence with thanksgiving; let us make a joyful noise to Him with songs of praise. (Ps. 95:2 AB)

In My Own Words

When I feel lonely, I can worship God and know that I am not alone because He is with me.

Something Fun to Do

Today would be a great day to sing a song to God and tell Him how much you love Him.

Here are the words to the chorus of a song I like to sing. It's called "Step by Step" by Rich Mullins.

> Oh God, You are my God
> And I will ever praise You.
> Oh God, You are my God
> And I will ever praise You.
> I will seek You in the morning
> And I will learn to walk in Your ways.
> And step by step You'll lead me
> And I will follow You all of my days.

God is always with us, but sometimes we don't notice. Worshipping God is really just choosing your thoughts! Worshipping God is different for everybody. My mom worships just by sitting quietly and watching the sunrise. She says it reminds her that God is faithful and full of beauty. My dad likes to worship God by listening to worship music. My dance teacher worships God when she dances. Just do something that causes you to appreciate God and celebrate how amazing He is, and you will be worshipping God.

Choose Your Thoughts

The next time you feel like no one cares about you or you just feel lonely, try worshipping God. It doesn't matter what you do to worship God as long as it keeps you focused on how good He is and how much

He loves you. Once you are focused on those two things, everything else will fall into place! You will feel loved, not lonely.

Now It's Your Turn!

Write Psalm 95:2 in your own words or copy it out of your favorite Bible translation.

Something to Think About
Yet I am not alone, because the Father is with Me. (John 16:32 AB)

In My Own Words
I am never alone, because God is always with me.

Something Fun to Do
Let's do a little experiment.

1. Take a big breath. Notice it coming in and going out.
2. Do you hear the sound your breath makes?
3. How does your body feel when you take that big breath in?
4. How does it feel to let that big breath out?

You are always breathing, but you don't always notice it, right? Well, God is like that. He is always with you. He always wants to speak to you, to love you, and to help you, but you might not notice.

Choose Your Thoughts
The next time you feel alone, take a deep breath and notice how it feels. Remind yourself that God is always with you, even when you can't tell. He is with you like breathing. You don't have to do anything to get Him to show up; He's already there! You just have to notice. God is always with you. The more you notice Him, the better you'll feel!

Now It's Your Turn!
Write John 16:32 in your own words or copy it out of your favorite Bible translation.

Lesson 7

What to Do When You Feel Discouraged

Hi, it's me, Emily. Today, I have to finish a presentation for my class. It's all about plants. We have to show our plants in pictures from books or the Internet. We have to tell about our plants. Then, we have to answer questions about them. We have to have a big presentation board with colored papers and things that make our plants interesting to the class. We are supposed to do all of the work at home—without help.

But that's the problem! I really need help, and that's exactly what I told my mom. "I can't do this by myself, Mom."

You know what she said?

"I don't want to hear *can't* from you, Emily. You have Jesus in you, and with Him you can do anything."

Today is different! I'm pretty sure that even with Jesus, I can't do this.

"Mom, I need you to help me," I said while I tried to look up more information about plants on the computer.

"Emily, Ms. Michaels said this is your project. You are supposed to do the project without help from your parents."

"But, Mom," I begged. "Sierra's mom totally helped her. You can tell. She has all kinds of stuff on her board."

"Emily, you don't know that. Sierra may have done a lot of hard work on her own."

"No, she didn't," I argued. "She even *said* her mom helped her!"

Mom wasn't looking at me. She was washing dishes in the sink. But I saw her shake her head like she does when she's disappointed. "Well, that's too bad. Sierra is supposed to do her own work. Anyway, you are not Sierra, and I am not Sierra's mother. Ms. Michaels wants you to do your own work on this project, and I know you can do it."

"Ugh. Mom." I crossed my arms and stared at her back. Sometimes she makes me so angry! "But I can't." I looked at the ceiling. I squeezed my hand into a fist. "I just can't do this by myself! I have been working on it all night! I worked on it all day yesterday. It took up my whole weekend!"

"I believe in you, Emily. You are smart, and you are capable. You can do this." Mom finished the dishes and walked over to stand beside me. She picked up the information pages I had already made. My pages were okay, but they weren't as long or as pretty as Sierra's. "This looks very good, Emily," Mom said as she read over my work. "I'm impressed."

"But, Mom." I looked up at her with my sweetest face. "I really want you to help me."

"Emily, this has to be your own work."

"But I can't do it!" I moaned and dropped my head on the table. My forehead pressed against my papers. I could see the tiny fibers of the page beneath my nose. "It's too hard."

"Emily. Remember what I said about the word *can't*." Mom brushed my hair with her fingers. I kept staring into the black and white ink on the page. Sierra's presentation was in color.

"Yes, ma'am." I sighed.

"Okay, then," she said. "I guess you'd better get busy." I didn't lift my head from the table. "Emily?" Mom said my name in the way she does when she wants me to get started with something and I'm not doing it.

"Okay." I sat up. "But I just don't think I can do this!" Why wouldn't she help me?

"Aha! Now you know what your problem is!" Mom clapped her hands together. "You don't *think* you can do this!" She smiled at me. "I'm pretty sure you know how to solve that problem."

"It's too dark to go to the tree house," I argued. "And I have to go into the tree house to change my thoughts."

Mom laughed. "Oh, Emily, now you're just being ridiculous!" I shut my mouth together really tight to keep from laughing. Mom was right. I did not have to be in the tree house to change my thoughts. I could sit right there at the kitchen table and do it. I know my questions by heart.

"Start thinking, Emily," Mom said as she walked out of the room.

So there I was, sitting at the table and staring at the computer and the big stack of books in front of me. I couldn't do it. I didn't want to do this. "Emily, get busy. It's getting late!" I heard Mom call from the laundry room.

I sat back in my chair. I wiggled my toes and squeezed my eyes shut tight. I said to myself, "Prepare to think." Then, I started with the first question: "Does God love me?" I stopped. I thought. "Yes, God loves me. The Bible says God loves me. I've read it lots of times. Thank you, God, for loving me."

Okay, second question. "What does God say about this?" Hmm. This is a little harder without my list. I wiggled my toes and squeezed my eyes shut even tighter. I stopped. I thought. I could picture the list in my head, but I couldn't see exactly what it said. I prayed and asked God to help me. Wait! That was it! I could ask God to help me! That's what it says! God will help me!

Now, the third question. "Do I believe what God says about me is true?" God says He will help me, and if that's true, then what did I need to do?

Hmm, it looked like I would have to make a decision. I had to choose my thoughts.

What would I choose to think about? I stopped. I thought. I wiggled just my left toes and then my right. God can do anything. He is so much bigger than I am. He made the plants. He understands them. He promised to help me understand things when I ask Him. The Bible says that I can do anything with God helping me. If that's true—and deep down inside, I know it is because I know God loves me and I know He tells the truth—then even though this project is really hard and it would be easier if Mom helped me, I am supposed to do the work by myself. With God's help, I can do anything. I can choose my thoughts, and that means I can choose my feelings. It was time to decide. What would I choose to think about? I closed my eyes and wiggled my toes. I chose to think about and believe what God says. He loves me, and He would help me. So instead of thinking I couldn't, I chose to think I could!

What about you? Do you have a story about a time when you felt like you couldn't do something? What did you do?

Something to Think About

May He grant you out of the rich treasury of His glory to be strengthened and reinforced with mighty power in the inner man, by the Holy Spirit (Himself indwelling your innermost being and personality). (Eph. 3:16 AB)

In My Own Words

Because God is living in me, I can do anything God calls me to do!

Something Fun to Do

Okay, this one is super easy. You'll need a paper lunch bag and a working flashlight.

1. Take the bag and the flashlight into a room that doesn't have a lot of light.
2. Put the flashlight inside the bag.
3. Turn on the flashlight.

See how the bag glows? The flashlight changes the bag from the inside! The bag doesn't light up by itself. We are the same way. God changes us from the inside, too! When God lives inside of us, His light shines through us. The Bible says the Holy Spirit lives in the very deepest part of who we are—you know, the part that makes you "you." That's where the Holy Spirit comes to live when we ask Jesus to be our Savior.

The Holy Spirit gives us strength and ability. As you choose to think God's kind of thoughts and listen to the Holy Spirit within you, the Holy Spirit will shine through you just like the flashlight shines through the bag. Trust the Holy Spirit within you and follow Him. He will do the rest.

Choose Your Thoughts

The next time you feel like you can't do something, remember that God, through His Holy Spirit, lives inside of you. He promises to strengthen you and help you do everything He calls you to do.

Now It's Your Turn!

Write Ephesians 3:16 using your own words or copy it out of your favorite Bible translation.

Something to Think About
Be strong and let your heart take courage, all you who hope in the Lord. (Ps. 31:24 NASB)

In My Own Words
I am counting on God, so I don't have to be discouraged. I know God will help me!

Something Fun to Do
Here's how I like to make myself feel strong and full of courage.

1. Stand tall, with your arms spread out really wide.
2. Plant your feet wide beneath you. Do you feel strong?
3. Now run and do your highest leap! Be sure that you land with your shoulders back and your head up high. Did that make you feel strong? It makes me feel strong.

What else can you do that makes you feel strong?

Sometimes it's hard for me to feel strong and full of courage when I have to do something that seems really hard or scary. Feeling strong and full of courage is easier when I remember to trust God. That's what being courageous is all about—doing something even if you've never done it before or it seems a little scary. As long as you are following God, He will be with you. As long as God is with you, He will help you. So be brave! God is bigger than any problem you will ever face!

Choose Your Thoughts
The next time you feel discouraged, remember to hold your head up high and put your shoulders back. You can be full of hope and courage because you trust in God and He is with you!

Now It's Your Turn!
Write Psalm 31:24 in your own words or copy it out of your favorite Bible translation.

Something to Think About

For You are my hope; O Lord God, You are my trust from my youth and the source of my confidence. (Ps. 71:5 AB)

In My Own Words

I feel good about me because God loves me and will help me.

Something Fun to Do

1. Grab your crayons and some paper.
2. Draw a picture of yourself and make sure it's pretty big, maybe about the size of one whole page.
3. Draw a heart inside of your body.
4. Color your heart in with your favorite color.
5. Now imagine that the color from your heart spreads throughout your whole body, from the top of your head to the tips of your toes.
6. Color in the body until your drawing is completely full of color.

Confidence begins in your heart, in what you believe about yourself. Think about how you colored your heart in and then the color spread throughout your whole body. It's the same way with confidence! Having confidence means believing in yourself. We can have confidence and believe in ourselves because we know God loves us and lives in us. Getting your confidence from God means that it starts on the inside, in your heart, just like in your drawing. And do you know the best thing about getting your confidence from God? No one can take it away from you!

Choose Your Thoughts

The next time you feel like something is too hard or like you aren't as good at something as someone else, choose to think about what God says about you. Make God your source of hope and confidence! You can read through this book and find Bible verses that tell you that God is always with you. He has good plans for you, and He wants to work everything out for your good. So choose to think about what God says about you and believe in yourself. God loves you so much! Let His love give you confidence.

Now It's Your Turn!

Write Psalm 71:5 in your own words or copy it out of your favorite Bible translation.

Lesson 8

Uh-oh: What to Do When You Make a Mistake and Feel Guilty!

(This is a curious question about feeling guilty because I've made a few mistakes. Hasn't everybody?)

Today, I really messed up. I was so mean to Mom. I even told her that I didn't like her being with me. I told her I just wanted her to get out of my room! I am so mad at myself for how I acted. I knew it was wrong even when I did it. I knew that I would feel bad about it later. But she just made me so mad! I wanted to be by myself. I guess I could have gone to my tree house, but she would have followed me out there.

It all started because I wanted Grace and Jenna to spend the night. I haven't had a sleepover at my house since last year! I have been waiting forever! Mom always says that we are too busy. She said last year that this year would be better. It isn't! Well, it's almost October, and I still haven't gotten to have a sleepover.

We planned it all out at school. We were gonna roast marshmallows and read our books using flashlights. Grace was going to bring her joke book, but Mom had to go and rain all over our parade. She said Dad did not have time to build a fire tonight and that it was going to rain, so camping out was a bad idea. Then she remembered that she had a party to bake for and had to get started right away. My house is so boring! Grace and Jenna will probably camp out at Jenna's house without me.

Anyway, that's why I was so mad at Mom. Now, not only am I

disappointed about the sleepover, but I also feel really guilty about how I treated Mom. I mean, I guess I should have just been okay when she said no. But I have been waiting since last year! A whole, entire summer has gone by without a single sleepover. That is pretty much unfair, right? I thought so, too. I told her it wasn't fair. I told her that she never cared about what I wanted and that I always had to play by myself while all of my friends were having fun. I told her that I didn't even want her to be in my room. I think I might have even been yelling at that point. Pretty mean things to say, I guess, especially when I know they aren't even true.

After I said all of that, Mom just looked at me. She looked at me and then turned around and walked out the door. Even though that is what I'd said I wanted her to do, I felt sad and lonely when she left. I still feel sad and lonely. I feel guilty too. I know I was wrong. My mom works really hard, and so does my dad. I play with my friends all the time. Maybe we don't have sleepovers, but we have fun. Every afternoon either I am at Grace's house or she comes to mine. It's like we're sisters!

Buddy, my sweet little parakeet, started singing in his cage. He sits on his swing and whistles while he looks out the window. I bet he wants to fly out of his cage straight out the window and into the sky. But he can't. Sometimes I let him fly around in my room. I decided today would be a good day to let Buddy loose.

"C'mon, boy," I said. I opened the tiny door for him to fly out.

He sat on the swing and chirped at me. He shifted back and forth on his little bird feet, the claws opening and closing with each step.

"Buddy, you can come out!" I tried to coax him out with my happiest voice. "C'mon, boy. Come out!"

He fluffed his feathers out and looked at me. But he didn't move from his swing.

"Buddy, don't you want out of your cage?" I asked. But I guess he didn't, so I just closed the door.

I looked out the window. I kinda felt like I was in a cage too. I felt like I was stuck in there all by myself. I missed my friends, and I missed my mom. I love my mom, and I didn't mean to hurt her feelings. Ugh. I really messed up!

The clouds were all swirly in the sky. It was gray and blue, all mixed together—not my favorite kind of sky. The trees moved in the wind. They reminded me of God. I recognized that I needed to choose my thoughts. I hadn't really thought about that! But that's just it. Thoughts are sneaky. I looked out the window again, and then I looked over at Buddy sitting on his swing. All of the sudden, I realized something. Buddy doesn't feel trapped! I do! I am trapped by my own feelings! I didn't want to spend the whole weekend in there alone, feeling sorry for myself and feeling guilty that I was so mean to Mom. (Of course, I didn't really want to apologize either. That's kind of embarrassing.)

Yep. It was definitely time to choose my thoughts.

So, what should I do first? You're right! I had to ask myself the first and most important question: "Does God love me?"

I think we both know the answer to that one. Yes! God loves us!

Then it was time for the second question: "How does God see me?" Hmm. Let's prepare to think.

What do I do to prepare to think?

I close my eyes and wiggle my toes, and I ask myself, "How does God see me?" As I think, I remember that God sees me as perfectly me, Emily. He sees me as His child. He loves me. But wait—what about when I do something bad, like yelling at my mom? Does He still love me? Well, I know He still loves me, but maybe He is a little, teeny tiny bit disappointed in me. Maybe He doesn't really like me much right now?

I wiggled my toes a little harder, and I closed my eyes really, really tight. How does God see me? God sees me as whole and complete. He has given me a perfect relationship with Him through Jesus. God sees me just the way He sees Jesus. When Jesus died for me, He took all of my mistakes and all of my guilt. He took every bad thing I have ever done and every bad thing I will ever do, so I don't have to feel guilty. I can feel God's love for me instead! And you know what that makes me want to do? Go and love my mom. I don't have to be embarrassed to apologize. I know I was wrong. I was wrong, but I know God forgives me. So I know it's okay to try again. I'm free, and my feelings cannot trap me! I was so excited that I had to run downstairs to find Mom.

"Mom!" I called her before I even got to the kitchen. "Mom!"
"Yes, Emily?"

I ran to her as fast as I possibly could. (I'm pretty fast!) As soon as I got to her, I wrapped my arms around her. I squeezed her tight and closed my eyes. I love the smell of her! She smells like cookies and flowers, two of my most favorite things. "I love you, Mom! I am so sorry I was mean to you!" I told her, and I pressed my face against her back.

"I love you too, sweetheart. You are my Emily. Thank you for saying you're sorry. It makes me feel better." Mom kissed my head, right on top, the way she always does. Right then, in that second, Mom and I were up in the clouds together. The sky was very, very, perfectly blue, and I was free.

Have you ever felt guilty about messing up? What did you choose to do?

Something to Think About

Forgetting the past and looking forward to what lies ahead, I press on to reach the end of the race and receive the heavenly prize for which God, through Christ Jesus, is calling us. (Phil. 3:13-14 NLT)

In My Own Words

When I make a mistake, I ask God to forgive me and I try again, because with Jesus, nothing is impossible.

Something Fun to Do

1. Find a backpack or another bag in your house.
2. Ask a grown-up to help you fill it with some heavy things you can drag around. I used cans of soup and tuna fish. Heavy books work really well!
3. Once it's super heavy, put one of your feet through the bag's straps.
4. Try and walk. Let the bag drag on the floor behind you.
5. After you have walked dragging the bag for a little while, take the bag off and walk without it.

Isn't that easier? When you keep thinking about everything you've done wrong, it's just like dragging that bag around. You end up feeling bad about yourself. You forget all of the good things God says about you. Everything feels too hard. But when you remember that Jesus took your place, you can let go of your mistakes. It's like Jesus came along and picked up your bag, and you don't have to carry it anymore! So just let Jesus have your mistakes. He's big enough to carry them.

Choose Your Thoughts

The next time you feel bad because you made a mistake or did something wrong, ask God to forgive you if you disobeyed His Word. If you need to apologize to someone, do that, too. But then, let Jesus have the bag! Choose to think the same thoughts God does—He thinks about how much He loves you. He doesn't even remember your mistakes. Look at Hebrews 8:12 and see for yourself! He has already forgiven you, and He chooses not to think about it anymore.

Now It's Your Turn!

Write Philippians 3:13-14 in your own words or copy it out of your favorite Bible translation.

Something to Think About

For by grace you have been saved through faith; and that not of yourselves, it is the gift of God. (Eph. 2:8 NASB)

In My Own Words

Salvation is a gift from God to me.

Something Fun to Do

Have you ever helped out around the house without being asked? Have you ever just given someone a little gift for no reason?

1. Today, I want you to think about something you can do for someone else or give to someone else that they will enjoy. It can be anything. One time I rearranged all of the canned foods in our pantry so that they were nice and neat. Mom really liked that! Another time, I played with my parakeet, Buddy, for an extra five minutes instead of watching TV. It can be something very small.
2. But you have to do it without expecting anything back. Just do it because you love the other person.

How did that feel? What did you choose to do?

When God forgave our sins through Jesus' death on the cross, He did it because He loves us and because He did not want us to live separated from His presence. It was a gift from God to us. God knows we need Him. He made us that way on purpose! All we have to do is accept the love He offers. You can't earn it. You don't need to "get" God to love you because He already does.

Choose Your Thoughts

The next time you catch yourself doing the "right" thing because you want God to be happy with you, stop and remember that God is *already* happy with you! He wants you to do the right thing because you trust Him and you believe He knows what's best for you, not because you want Him to love you. When you believe that God treasures you, you will do what He tells you because you know He only wants what's best for you. You will do what He tells you out of love and honor for God, not because you're afraid of Him. When we are afraid of someone, we hide from them. God doesn't want you to hide from Him. He wants you to run to Him, especially when you're in trouble, because, guess what—He is the only one who can really help you! It's like this—love and honor for God bring joy and peace. Fear just brings more fear.

The next time you are choosing your thoughts and trying to make the best decision, remember that God already loves you. When you know He loves you, you will follow Him with joy and peace.

Now It's Your Turn!

Write Ephesians 2:8 in your own words or copy it out of your favorite Bible translation.

Something to Think About
And their sins and their lawless deeds I will remember no more. (Heb. 10:17 NASB)

In My Own Words
God does not remember my sins. For Him, it's like they never happened.

Something Fun to Do

1. Grab a piece of paper.
2. Think of a time when you messed up and didn't do the right thing.
3. Write it down on the piece of paper.
4. Now, take a big eraser and erase it! Yep. Erase the whole thing until you can't see it anymore.

That is what God does with our sins. He tells us that He will remember them no more. He is never going to bring them back up. He is not going to punish you because Jesus took the punishment for every sin that anyone will ever commit. So, as far as God is concerned, you have a clean page to write on! What do you want to say? I decided to write *loved, precious,* and *happy* on my page!

Choose Your Thoughts
The next time you feel badly about something you've done or you feel like maybe God might stop loving you, just think about Jesus. Jesus died so that you would never, ever, no way, no how, be separated from God's love! Remember? And that means that all of your mistakes, no matter what kind they are or how many there are, will ever be enough to stop God from loving you. He has chosen to remember them no more.

Now It's Your Turn!
Write Hebrews 10:17 in your own words or copy it out of your favorite Bible translation.

Lesson 9

What to Do When You Don't Know What to Do

I have to make a decision. I guess it wouldn't be that big of a deal, except that I have to choose. I have to choose whether I want to take art or dance. I can't do both. I'm pretty disappointed because it is pretty much impossible to choose between art and dance. Mom says that if I don't take dance, it won't mean I stop being a dancer. I guess that's true, but I really like all of my friends at dance class. And this year, I was going to get to make up my own dance and perform it on stage, all by myself!

The thing is, there is a brand new art studio in town, and they sent out a little flyer at school. They teach all kinds of art. They teach pottery and painting. They make a different project every week! I really, really want to learn to make pottery. Lydia had her birthday party there, and everyone said that the art teacher was super nice.

This is so hard! If I don't take dance, all my friends will dance without me. I won't be in the recital or anything. I won't get to be in the Christmas parade either. I love the Christmas parade because Miss Suzanne, my teacher, always serves hot chocolate and sugar cookies. And that reminds me—if I don't dance, I won't get the sweatshirt everyone gets when they're in the Christmas parade! I will miss out on *everything*! Except art, I guess. I will get to take art.

I have to decide before Friday because next week is when the art classes start. I asked my mom if I could try the art classes. That way I could see what I think before I decide. She said that once we sign up, we're signed up and I can't change my mind.

Obviously, it was time to think, so I climbed up the ladder to my tree house—red step, yellow step, purple step, blue step, yellow step, red step, and finally, purple step. I stopped to look around. I could see over our fence into Mr. Raley's yard. He was working in his garden. I could even see three yards over. When I looked the other way, I could almost see into Grace's yard. I guess I would still see Grace if I didn't go to dance, but I wouldn't see everybody else. I pushed open the little wooden door. My papers and crayons were all over the table where I left them. I walked over to my Thinking Book. It was time to make a decision! I had to choose my thoughts.

First question: Does God love me? That's an easy one! Of course He does. I'm His child, and He loves me no matter what.

Second question: How does God see me? Does God see me as a dancer? Does God see me as an artist? Does God want me to take dance or art this year? Hmm. How does God see me? I looked at my List of Thoughts Worth Thinking. God sees me as His child, loved and cherished. He sees me as righteous, whole and complete, in a perfect relationship with Him. He sees me as sanctified, and that means He has a special purpose for me. He says He is always with me. He says that He will lead me and guide me.

None of the things on my list helped me know whether to take dance or art. This was pretty confusing. I decided Mom was going to have to help me. I grabbed my Thinking Book and climbed back down the ladder. I stepped over Roxy on my way through the door.

"Hey, girl," I said. I patted her on the head and scratched behind her furry ears. She looked up at me with a happy doggy smile. I called out for Mom, but she was not in the kitchen.

"What d'ya need, Punkin?" It was Dad. I followed his voice into the living room. He was sitting in his chair, checking e-mail and watching the news.

"Well, I need some help," I told him, and I plopped down on the arm of his chair. Dad wrapped his long arm around me for a hug. "What seems to be the problem, Baby Girl?" Dad always calls me little pet names, unless I'm in trouble.

"Mom says I have to choose," I said in my saddest voice. Maybe Dad would feel sorry for me. "She says it's either dance or art class," I said.

"Hmm. Tough choice." He nodded and looked at me over the top of his glasses. He wiggled his dark eyebrows and gave me a sideways look. "What're ya gonna choose?"

I rolled my eyes. *Great*, I thought. *He isn't going to help me!*

"Dad," I said, "I don't *want* to choose."

"I know." He smiled and squeezed me tight. "That's why it's a tough choice."

I just looked at him and frowned. He didn't understand. "I see you've got your Thinking Book," he said. "Have you been trying to choose your thoughts?"

"Yes," I said, and I let out a big sigh. It made my bangs fly off of my face. "But it didn't help." I told him, "I know God loves me. I know how He sees me. But that doesn't tell me whether I should take dance or art." If I were really honest, I would have told Dad that I was a little mad at God for not making this easier on me. I mean, why couldn't I just do both?

"Guess you're probably a little mad at God about this, huh?" Dad said. I guess he's a mind reader.

I looked at my shoes. "Well, I did pray that He would let me do both." I was a little embarrassed to admit this.

"Hmm," Dad said. "I'm pretty sure that isn't going to happen."

"I know. I know," I interrupted. "Mom already told me. I have to choose."

"Tell me again," Dad said. "What did you say about knowing how God sees you?"

"I know how God sees me."

"You do?"

"Yes, Dad." I looked at him like he was crazy and held up my Thinking Book. "It's all right here!"

"Okay, show me."

I opened the book to the List of Thoughts Worth Thinking and handed it to Dad. He took the book and made room for me to squeeze in next to him in the big chair. He adjusted his glasses and began to read to himself. "Hmm."

"What is it?" I asked.

"Well, this says that God will lead you in the right direction."

"Exactly!" I said. "But He isn't."

"Well, how do you think God leads you?" Dad asked me.

I thought about it. "By His Word, I guess."

"Nice answer, but what does it mean?" Dad grinned at me. I hate it when he grins like that. He knows he's got me.

"That if I read my Bible, it will tell me what to do?" I tried to sound sure, but it ended up sounding like a question.

Dad gently smoothed my hair. "Oh, my little girl, if it were only that easy," he said. "The Bible is not a magic book. The Bible tells you who you are in Jesus. It tells you who God is and what things look like from His perspective," Dad explained, and then he pointed a finger at my heart. "And when you know who you are to God and you know how much He loves you, you make decisions based on that. And decisions based on God's love for you are always the best decisions."

I laid my head back on Dad's chest and listened to his heartbeat. God loves me even more than my dad does. He loves me more than I can understand, but I can feel it, like I can feel my dad's heartbeat. I can trust God because I know He loves me and only has good things for me. I closed my eyes and wiggled my toes. I stopped. I thought. It was time to make a decision. The only decision I really had to make was whether I believe God. Do I believe God is who He says He is? Do I believe God loves me like He says He does? And if all that's true, then I can choose art or I can choose dance. Either way, it will work out just right because that is how good God is to me!

"I've made my decision," I told Dad.

"What did you decide?" he asked, his voice rumbling in his chest and tickling my ear.

"I decided to trust God." I looked up at Dad, and he smiled at me.

"That's the best decision you can make, sweetheart. I'm so proud of you."

I gave him a quick kiss on the cheek and jumped out of the chair. "I have to go now!" I said and skipped toward the door.

"Where are you going?" Dad asked with a laugh.

"To see if I can dance and paint at the same time!" I yelled as I ran out the door.

Now, it's your turn. Have you ever had to make a tough choice? How did you decide what to do?

Something to Think About

But when He, the Spirit of Truth (the Truth-giving Spirit) comes, He will guide you into all the Truth. (John 16:13 AB)

In My Own Words

God will help me know the truth.

Something Fun to Do

1. Create a secret path through your yard or your house. Mark the beginning and then, at the end, place a small treasure.
2. Ask a friend or family member if he or she would like you to show them the way to the treasure.
3. Begin at the starting place and then take the other person by the hand. Lead him or her through the secret path until you reach the treasure.

God has created a way for you to know all of the things that you need to know. He has given you the Holy Spirit, who will lead you in the right direction. Just like you led the other person right to the treasure, God will always lead you right where you need to go. And guess what? If you make a mistake, you don't have to worry. God is always with you, and He knows exactly where you are! If you stop following Him and get lost or make a mistake, God will get you right back on track!

Choose Your Thoughts

The next time you feel confused about something, ask the Holy Spirit to lead you into truth. God's truth will help you figure everything out. He can help you make decisions. He can help you understand your feelings. And this is really important—He can even help you choose your thoughts!

Now It's Your Turn!

Write John 16:13 in your own words or copy it out of your favorite Bible translation.

Something to Think About

Trust in the Lord with all of your heart and do not lean on your own understanding. In all your ways acknowledge Him and He will make your paths straight. (Prov. 3:5-6 NASB)

In My Own Words

I have to trust what God says more than what I see.

Something Fun to Do

1. Make a few little bugs out of clay or rolled-up paper. They can be any color or shape, but make sure they are really, really tiny.
2. Then, take them outside.
3. Find a little spot in the grass that you can turn into a city for your bugs. You can add some little rocks for buildings. You can even make some buildings out of clay or cardboard if you want to.
4. Put the buildings and the bugs in the grass to make your city.
5. Next, lie down in the grass and imagine that you are one of the tiny bugs. What do you see? I pretend I am a teeny, tiny ladybug. The pieces of grass are as tall as big trees to me. When I look between the pieces of grass, it's like looking into a forest.
6. After you have gotten your bug's-eye view, stand back up. Look down at your imaginary bug city. It looks pretty different now, right? You can see so much more than you could when you were just a little, itty-bitty bug.

God is so much bigger than we are. He can see things we cannot. I think He sees our lives sort of the way you see your little city when you stand up. You can see more than you could when you were on the ground. It is the same way with God. But God knows what it's like to be small, living in the little city too, because Jesus came to Earth and lived as a man. That's why it's better to listen to God and follow His directions. Our ability to see and understand things is limited by how small we are, even when we become adults. But God is limitless and sees everything, so we can trust Him. We do not have to try and figure everything out for ourselves.

Choose Your Thoughts

The next time you have to make a decision, remember to ask God for help. And remember, whatever you decide, you want to be in harmony with God and His way of being. That is sure to put you in the best possible place!

Now It's Your Turn!

Write Proverbs 3:5-6 in your own words or copy it out of your favorite Bible translation.

Something to Think About

And He said to him, "You shall love the Lord your God with all your heart, and with all your soul, and with all your mind." This is the great and foremost commandment. (Matt. 22:37-38 NASB)

In My Own Words

The most important thing for me to do is to love God.

Something Fun to Do

1. Draw a heart on a piece of paper.
2. Now, draw some curvy lines through it so that your heart is divided into three or four sections, like a puzzle.
3. Color in one section of your heart puzzle. You can use whatever color you want. I used red.
4. Okay, color in one more section. How does it look? Have you colored in your whole heart? You should have a section or two left to color.
5. Now, color in all of the sections until your heart is complete.

Jesus said that the most important command was to love God with all of your heart, all of your mind, and all of your soul. I think that means to love God in every part of your life, in every way you can. Just like your heart puzzle had more than one part, there are different parts of your life. God wants you to fill up each part of your life with love for Him.

Choose Your Thoughts

The more you think about how good God is and how much He loves you, the more you will love Him. The more you love God, the more you will follow God. The more you follow God, the better your life will be. It's that simple. Choose your thoughts. Choose your life.

Now It's Your Turn!

Write Matthew 22:37-38 using your own words or copy it out of your favorite Bible translation:

Lesson 10

What to Do When You're Worried

One afternoon it was time for dance. I raced all over the house looking for my tap shoes. I couldn't find them. There was *no way* I was gonna tell Mom. We'd already had to buy a new pair once this year. I try to keep up with things, but it's just too hard for me sometimes! I was running around the house looking everywhere they could possibly be, but I couldn't find them anywhere! I knew that Mom was going to be upset with me for losing my shoes again. I was really worried.

I looked in the coat closet. I searched twice under my bed. I even pulled out all the stuffed animals and socks and books that had slipped down between the bed and the wall, but my tap shoes weren't there. I checked my dance bag, and they weren't in there either. (That's where they are supposed to be.) I tried really, really hard to remember the last time I had worn them.

"Emily, are you ready to go?" Mom called from the stairs.

"Almost," I answered, and I shoved all of my shoes back into my closet—no tap shoes there.

"Emily." Mom's voice was on the edge of being upset. "We need to go!"

I really didn't want to tell her that I couldn't find them. What would she say? She would probably lecture me about being irresponsible.

What if I never find my tap shoes and Mom and Dad say I can't have any more? I won't be able to take tap. I love tap. *I love my tap teacher, Miss Amy. What will Miss Amy say when she finds out? She will probably be disappointed in me!*

I checked every one of my bags and backpacks. Maybe they were in my tree house!

"Emily, let's go!" Mom said. She sounded angry. "Now."

I ran down the stairs. "One second, Mom!" I shouted as I raced past her, through the doorway, and into the backyard. "I have to check something!"

"No, ma'am," she said. "We have to leave now!"

I just kept going up the ladder. My shoes had to be in there! I was going to be in trouble with Mom for not listening. I knew she would be mad. But at least I would have my shoes! And there they were, right in the middle of the floor where I'd left them. What a relief!

"I'm coming, Mom!" I called as loudly as I could, hurrying down the ladder. Mom was standing at the door, and she was not happy.

"Emily, you have disobeyed me. We are late. You lose your TV time today and tomorrow."

"Okay," I said quietly as I followed her to the car.

"What was so important that you decided to disobey me?" Mom asked as we pulled out of the driveway.

"Well," I hesitated. I hated to tell her because I knew she would be even angrier with me.

"I, uh, I couldn't find my tap shoes." I said it as quickly as I could. "But I found them! They were in my tree house!" I held them toward the front seat so that she could see them dangling over her shoulder.

"Why didn't you tell me?" she asked. "Maybe I could have helped you find them and we wouldn't have been late."

"I was worried that you would be mad."

"Well, I might have gotten mad, but we would have found them and we wouldn't have been late," Mom said. "I understand that you were worried about making me mad. But I still love you, and I could have helped you find your shoes."

"I'm sorry I didn't tell you."

"I'm sorry you had to worry about making me mad. Worrying never helps solve anything, but we all do it," Mom told me as we stopped at the stoplight. "It's sort of like this stoplight. Worrying keeps you on yellow all of the time. You can never really move forward with confidence. You're always waiting to see if the light will turn red.

You can rush forward and hope to beat it, but either way, you can't feel sure." The light changed to green and Mom drove the car forward. "I bet you were pretty miserable, worrying all afternoon about finding your shoes."

"Yes, ma'am." I nodded. "I'm definitely putting them back in their bag from now on! Then, I won't have to worry."

"Right. But even if you do make a mistake and then you start to worry, there *is* something else you can do."

"Choose my thoughts?" I asked.

"Choose your thoughts," she said with a nod. "What would that have been like today?"

"Well, I guess I would have started with the first question: does God love me?" I answered.

"And what do you think the answer is?"

"I know God loves me," I said.

"How do you know God loves you?" Mom asked.

Of course, she already knew the answer! She just wanted me to think about it.

"The Bible tells me that God loves me, and God tells me He loves me when I ask Him," I told her.

"Good," she said. "What's next?"

"Well, I have to think about how God sees me."

"Right," Mom agreed. "So how does God see you?"

"Well," I said, and then I stopped. I had to think about that one. "He sees me as perfectly me. He sees me as His child. He loves me!"

"Exactly. So do you need to worry?"

I had to think for a minute. I wiggled my toes in my shoes and closed my eyes. "No! God says not to worry but to pray and to thank Him!" I shout.

"Good job, Emily! That was a hard one." Mom smiled at me over her shoulder. "Is that it?"

"Well, no ... then, I have to make a decision."

"Okay. What do you think you could have decided today?"

"Hmm." I pressed my lips together. "I think I would have decided not to worry."

"Good," Mom said. "Why not?"

"Because I know God loves me, and I know what He says is true. So I don't need to worry. I will pray to God for help and thank Him because I know He will help me with whatever I'm worried about. He will even help me not to worry!" I told her.

"I'm proud of you, Emily," Mom said as she turned off the car. "You really know how to choose your thoughts!"

That's my story! Why don't you tell me about a time when you were worried and had to choose *your* thoughts.

Something to Think About

Jesus said, "Do not be worried about your life…. Seek first His kingdom and His righteousness." (Matt. 6:25 and Matt. 6:33 NASB)

In My Own Words

I'm not going to worry. I'm going to think about God's way of thinking and living.

Something Fun to Do

1. Find a box that you can use as a drum. Try to pick one that makes a loud drumming noise. A hard box works better than a soft one, so a shoebox would be better than a cereal box.
2. Okay, start playing nice and slow. Boom. Boom. Boom. Boom.
3. Now stop.
4. Change it up, and make it faster. BoomBoomBoomBoom.

Did you hear the difference? Try making a different sound. Make it louder or softer. Try to play some songs that you know.

Sometimes we have worries that keep us from enjoying our day. Instead of worrying, Jesus says to think about God. He wants us think about how much God loves us. He wants us to think about how many good things God has planned for us. It's just like changing the sounds you made on your drum. Instead of playing slow, you played fast. Instead of playing loud, you played soft. Easy, right?

Choose Your Thoughts

The next time you start to worry, all you have to do is change the song. Stop playing the worry song and start playing a worship song. Tell God how good He is and how much you love Him. Pretty soon, you won't be worried at all!

Now It's Your Turn!

Write Matthew 6:25 and 6:33 in your own words or copy it out of your favorite Bible translation.

Something to Think About
The prayer of a righteous person is powerful and effective. (James 5:16 New International Version, NIV)

In My Own Words
My prayers are powerful and make a difference because I am completely accepted by God and He cares about me.

Something Fun to Do

1. Look around your house and find some empty boxes. I used cereal boxes and shoeboxes.
2. Find as many as you can.
3. Stack them up to make a wall or tower.
4. Now, stand back and imagine that the boxes are super strong like a brick wall.
5. You are going to kick the boxes down with one big kick. Get ready.
6. 1,2,3, *kick*!

Did the boxes fall down? Your kick was powerful and effective. It made a difference. It changed things. When you have problems or worries, you can pray. Praying is powerful and effective just like your kick. It can knock down all kinds of problems.

Choose Your Thoughts
The next time you have a problem, you can pray and talk to God. Your prayers are powerful, and they do make a difference.

Now It's Your Turn!
Write James 5:16 in your own words or copy it out of your favorite Bible translation.

Something to Think About

"For I know the plans I have for you," says the Lord. "They are plans for good and not for disaster, to give you a future and a hope." (Jer. 29:11 NLT)

In My Own Words

God has great things planned for me! It's gonna be awesome!

Something Fun to Do

1. Imagine you are planning a party for someone you love.
2. Now think ... What kind of party would you have? Would you have food? Would you play music? Would you plan the party to be inside or outside? What do you think makes a party fun? Would you invite a lot of people to the party or just a few? How would you decorate for the party? Would you have balloons or flowers? Would you decorate the door to your party?

God has planned your life the same way you planned the party. Think about how much you love the person you planned the party for—you wanted everything to be perfect for him or her, right? Well, God loves us, and He wants our lives to be like the best party ever. He created your future just for you! God has never made another you. You are the only one who can live your life. God has it all planned out, just like the party! He wants you to have friends. He wants you to laugh. He wants you to have fun. He even wants you to have presents! He wants you to feel loved. You're really special to God, and He has a special life planned for you—the biggest and best party ever!

Choose Your Thoughts

The next time you feel worried about what is happening in your life, stop and remember that God has a great plan for you. You may not be able to imagine or see it right now, but God is so much bigger than you. Don't worry about what you can't see. Trust God and He will lead you in the exact direction He wants you to go!

Now It's Your Turn!

Write Jeremiah 29:11 in your own words or copy it out of your favorite Bible translation.

Lesson 11

What to Do When You Feel Jealous

(This curious question is from a day when I was just a teensy-weensy bit jealous.)

One day, my friend Grace invited me to go swimming at her house. We were so excited when my mom said yes! We raced upstairs to my room to get my bathing suit. As soon as I had everything together, we took off on our bikes. Grace has a beautiful swimming pool in her backyard. It has a slide and a fountain.

Once we got there, we jumped in at the same time holding hands. We tried to make the smallest splash possible. Then we tried to make the biggest splash. Her mom gave us points for how big our splashes were, and I won! But, Grace wanted to have a diving contest. I'm not very good at diving. "Oh, come on, Emily. It will be fun!" Grace begged me. "Please." She made puppy-dog eyes. "Please?"

I looked at the ground. I'm scared of diving. "I don't really want to dive today."

Grace knows I don't like diving, but she got very excited. "I will teach you!" she said. "I promise! I will show you how, and then you will be so good at it!" I gave up and shrugged my shoulders.

"Okay," I said.

We tried and tried. Well, *I* tried. Grace stood there and told me what to do and how easy it should be. Every time I would mess up, she would stand on the edge, her toes all lined up nice and neat, and say, "Look, you do it like this!" Then, boom! She would dive right in—perfect, every time. I would try again, and smack! I would land right on the middle of my belly, every time. "Quit looking up, Emily!" Grace would say. "You have to keep looking down!" She would stand up, go to the edge of the pool, and say, "See, like me!" Then off she'd go again. Suddenly, I didn't like her very much.

"I think I'm going to go home," I said finally.

"No!" she said, "You haven't learned to dive! You have to learn to dive!"

"Grace, maybe you should play something else in the pool," her mom suggested, but I didn't want to play anything else. I just wanted to leave.

"No, thanks," I said. I tried to be polite. "I think I just want to go home." All the way home I kept thinking about how Grace had such a perfect dive and how it was so easy for her. It was probably because she had her own pool. I wished I had my own pool. I bet if I had my own pool, I would be able to dive too.

I was feeling pretty mad by the time I got home. When Mom asked if I had fun swimming, I told her it was okay. Actually, I was a little mad at Mom, too. If my parents would just get a pool, I could learn to dive even better than Grace. The phone rang, and I didn't even try to answer it. I just sat in my room and stared out the window at our boring backyard full of grass. "Emily," Mom said from the door, "it's Grace, and she wants to know if you want to come back over and play basketball." I shook my head and said, "No, thanks. She's probably better at basketball, too." Mom left the room, and I heard her say good-bye to Grace. Then she came back in. "Emily, did something happen that hurt your feelings today?"

"Yes. Grace is bossy. She thinks she knows everything about diving and wants to tell me what to do all the time."

"Tell me what happened." Mom sat on the edge of my bed.

"Well, we were swimming and having a jumping contest, and that was fun. Mrs. Williams judged our jumps. Then Grace wanted to have a diving contest. I didn't want to, but she kept begging me and begging me, so finally I said okay. Then all she did was keep diving and saying, 'See? This is how you do it! It's sooo easy.' Finally, I just came home." I was trying really hard not to let Mom see that I was about to cry.

Mom reached over and gave me a hug. I started crying anyway. "I wish we had a pool," I said into Mom's shoulder. "Why can't we get a pool? I want to be able to dive like Grace. If we had a pool, I know I could dive like her. It's not fair."

Mom kept patting my back. She smiled at me and kissed my forehead. "I'm sorry you're frustrated. And I know you want what Grace has, but we have other things."

"But I really, really need a pool," I told her. "I want to be able to dive like Grace."

"Emily, do you like how you feel right now?" she asked.

"No, ma'am." I looked out the window. I felt miserable.

"Do you think that choosing your thoughts would help?"

I shrugged and sighed. "I guess," I said. I knew Mom was right, but I didn't feel like choosing better thoughts. I wanted a pool and to be able to dive like Grace.

"I love you, Emily Mason." Mom stood up and then bent down to look me in the eye. She put both of her hands on the sides of my face. "Look at me," she said. Then she said it. Yep, you know what she said—"Choose your thoughts. Choose your life."

So I went up in my tree house with my book of thoughts. It was under my big pile of dress-ups, as usual. I opened it to the first page. It says, "Choose your thoughts. Choose your life." I turned the page. "Does God love me?" That is always the first question I ask when I am choosing my thoughts. I stopped. I wiggled my toes and squeezed my eyes shut tight. "Prepare to think," I said to myself. I thought about how God loves me even when I am not very lovable, even when I feel jealous or angry. The Bible tells me that God loves me so much that He sent His Son to die for me. Yes, I believe God loves me. "Thank you God, for loving me," I told Him.

I turned the page. It said, "What does God say about me?" I stopped. I wiggled my toes and squeezed my eyes shut. I think. God says so many things about me that I can't remember them all. I turned to my list called "Things God Says About Me." I ran my finger down the page and stopped when I got to "God says He likes me just the way I am."

Looked like I would have to make a decision.

I turned the page. "What do I choose to think about?" I squeezed my eyes shut and wiggled my toes. The Bible says God loves me and has promised to take care of me. It also says God likes me just the way I am. I can choose my thoughts, and that means I can choose my feelings. It was time to decide. What would I choose to think about? I closed my eyes and wiggled my toes. Did I want to feel jealous and think about what I don't have or what I can't do? Or did I want to choose to think about what God says? I chose to think about what God says. He says I am loved, and I am perfect just the way I am.

What about you? Do you have a story about a time when you felt jealous?

Something to Think About

This High Priest of ours understands our weaknesses, for He faced all of the same testings we do, yet He did not sin. (Heb. 4:15 NLT)

In My Own Words

Jesus faced all of the same problems I do. He understands just how I feel, and He wants to help me.

Something Fun to Do

Today I want you to pretend to be someone else!

1. Decide who you want to be.
2. You can use your own dress-ups, like a hat or a crown or maybe an old dance costume.
3. I want you to pretend to be that person for an entire day!

The last time I played this game, I pretended to be Roxy. When I was pretending, I crawled around on the floor. I was going to take a drink out of her water bowl, but it was too gross! I decided it was better just to pretend. All I did was lie around all day. I was bored. I kept moving from the floor to the dog bed and then outside. Roxy followed me everywhere I went. I tried to get Mom to throw Roxy's Frisbee for me, but she said no. It was kind of a long day. I was happy when the day was over, and I got to sit at the table to eat my dinner instead of eating out of the dog bowl.

Pretending to be Roxy sure helped me to understand why she gets so excited whenever I want to play with her! It's boring just sitting around all day. And I know why she always gets in her dog bed, too. That floor is really hard! How about you? Did you discover something about the person or animal you pretended to be? Do you understand more about how they feel?

The Bible says that Jesus understands how we feel because He lived on Earth, too. He was a baby and a little boy before He was a man. Did you know He had to grow up just like you do? That's why we can go to Jesus with any problem we have and He understands. Jesus felt the same feelings that you feel, and He knows how to help you choose your thoughts. He's not disappointed with you when you have a problem. Jesus understands, and He loves you so much that He wants to help you. It's just like me with Roxy. I throw her Frisbee for her every day now because I love her and I know how she feels. I know she gets bored and lonely. So I help her. I understand.

Choose Your Thoughts

The next time you think no one understands, talk to Jesus. Jesus understands whatever you might be going through, and He wants to help you. All you have to do is let Him!

Now It's Your Turn!

Write Hebrews 4:15 in your own words or copy it out of your favorite Bible translation.

Something to Think About

You have searched me, Lord, and you know me.... You are familiar with all my ways. I praise you because I am fearfully and wonderfully made. (Ps. 139:1-14 NIV)

In My Own Words

God made me. He made me the way I am on purpose. I am thankful to God because He made me special.

Something Fun to Do

Today, you will need some clay.

1. Use your clay to build something.
2. It can be anything you want it to be. It can be a flower or a tree or a person, whatever you want!
3. Don't worry about making it perfect—art is for fun! I made a tree with red leaves and a purple trunk.
4. This is your very own masterpiece. It won't be like anyone else's because you made it. It will have just a little bit of your personality in it. That's what makes it special!

Just like you created your sculpture carefully and put a little bit of your personality into it, God created you carefully and made you in His image. You are God's very own masterpiece!

Choose Your Thoughts

The next time you feel jealous about what someone else can do or what that person has that you don't, remember that God made you the way you are on purpose! He loves you, and He is so happy with you. When you choose to think about how God created you with so much care and so much love, you will forget about what you don't have and see the amazing thing you do have—a relationship with the God who created the whole universe! How awesome is that?

Now It's Your Turn!

Write Psalm 139:1-14 in your own words or copy it out of your favorite Bible translation.

Something to Think About

A joyful heart is good medicine, but a broken spirit dries up the bones. (Prov. 17:22 NASB)

In My Own Words

Being happy is good for me!

Something Fun to Do

You are going to love this because it's all about the things you love! Today I want you to make a box of happiness. Here's how you do it:

1. Find a cardboard box and decorate the outside. You can add pictures or papers or anything else that glues on.
2. When the way your box looks makes you feel really, really happy, it's time to fill it up!
3. Go on a scavenger hunt for anything and everything that makes you feel happy.
4. If something doesn't fit in your box, you can always put a picture of it in your box. I have pictures of my family, Roxy, and a horse in my box. It doesn't matter that I don't have my own horse.

What did you find for your box?

All of the little things in your box of happiness are just things. By themselves, they can't make you happy. But they are reminders of some very important things—God is good, He loves you, and He has good plans for you. Your box of happiness will help you choose thoughts of joy. Thoughts of joy will help you feel better. They can even comfort you when you feel sad or angry or jealous.

Choose Your Thoughts

The next time you feel jealous, pull out your box of happiness. It will help you choose your thoughts. When you choose thoughts of happiness, you fill your heart with joy. Being happy is way better than being jealous. That's for sure!

Now It's Your Turn!

Write Proverbs 17:22 in your own words or copy it out of your favorite Bible translation.

Lesson 12

What to Do When Someone Hurts Your Feelings

(This was a really bad day.)

Today, my friends Jenna and Grace really hurt my feelings. When I went to play with them at recess, they whispered something and ran away from me. They were laughing with their friends from Mrs. Rodman's class, Annie and Lena. Lena said I couldn't play whatever they were playing. She said they already had enough people. Jenna acted like I wasn't even there. Grace didn't even stand up for me. I looked around for someone else to play with, but everybody was already playing with other friends. Jenna and Grace are supposed to be my friends. I would never do something like that to them! They really hurt my feelings.

The rest of the day I felt really bad. I kept thinking about how they had left me out and how they liked Annie and Lena better than me. When we went to art this afternoon, Jenna tried to talk to me, but I ignored her. Then Grace called my name and tried to catch up with me on the way to car line, but I just pretended that I didn't hear her. Why should I be nice to them after they had been so mean to me?

"How was school?" Mom asked when I got in the car.

"Okay," I said.

"That good, huh?" She looked back at me. "Sounds like maybe you had a yucky day?"

I twisted my mouth up against my nose. "I guess you could say that," I said.

"Did you have to do something hard in English?" Mom asked.

"No, not really." I shook my head and looked out the window.

Grace and her mom had pulled up next to us, and Grace was waving like crazy at me. I pretended not to see her.

"Emily, why are you ignoring Grace?" Mom asked as Mrs. Williams pulled past us into the street.

"I don't know," I said.

"You don't know why you're ignoring your best friend?"

"I wasn't ignoring her," I answered. "I just didn't feel like waving."

"Oh, I see," Mom said.

I knew she didn't. I knew she wanted me to talk about it, but I didn't feel like talking.

When we got home, I dropped my backpack on the kitchen table. "I don't have any homework today," I told her.

"Oh, lucky you! What are you going to do then?"

"I think I'm just gonna go play in my tree house," I said, and I headed straight for the door. I forgot my snack, so I had to turn around and grab two cookies from the counter. I love cookies. It doesn't matter that Mom makes them every day and that I've had them all my life. I love cookies! Peanut butter oatmeal chocolate chip is my favorite. Mom says that's because I can never choose just one thing. She's right! I grabbed my cookies and a glass of milk and headed outside.

"Hey, not so fast there, little missy! You know that you don't need to take one of my good glasses out to the tree house," Mom reminded me.

"Okay," I said, disappointed. I had been hoping to slip out without getting caught. I gulped down my milk and put my glass in the sink. "Thanks for the cookies." I took my cookies and headed for the tree house. I held them between my teeth as I climbed the ladder—red step, yellow step, purple step, blue step, and then yellow step, red step, and finally, purple step. I had barely made it to the top before the cookies fell apart.

Once I was inside, I sat down at my little table and ate my cookies. They didn't taste very good. I still felt pretty hurt about how my two friends—or two people I *thought* were my friends—had treated me.

They had really hurt my feelings, and then they had tried to talk to me, like I was gonna be all nice to them after they told me to go away on the playground.

I finished my cookies and looked around for something to do. *Who needs friends? I have my tree house,* I thought, *and my books, and God, too.* All of a sudden, my thoughts weren't making sense. Saying I don't need my friends because I have God? God says I should love my friends. "Really, God?" I asked Him, "even when I don't feel like it?"

I started thinking. Mom always says that changing my thoughts can change my feelings. "I guess I have to make a decision," I said out loud to myself.

I got up and pulled my Thinking Book out from under the humongous pile of dress-ups. I opened it to the first page. "Choose your thoughts. Choose your life." I turned the page, "Does God love me?" That's the first question. I stopped. I wiggled my toes and squeezed my eyes shut tight. I said to myself out loud, "Emily, prepare to think."

Does God love me? I asked myself.

Yes. The Bible tells me He loves me.

I closed my eyes and wiggled my toes and thought about just how much God loves me. Then I said, "Thank you, Jesus, for loving me. I love you."

I turned the page. "What does God say about me?" I stopped. I wiggled my toes and squeezed my eyes shut.

God says so many things about me, I thought.

I couldn't remember them all, so I turned to the "List of Thoughts Worth Thinking" page. I ran my finger down the list and stopped at, "God says I am loved and I should love others like He loves me." Then it hit me.

Wait a minute! God loves me, but He also loves Jenna and Grace and Lena and Annie.

I had to make a decision.

I turned the page. "What do I choose to think about?" I squeezed my eyes shut tight and wiggled my toes. I didn't feel like being loving toward Grace and Jenna. I didn't even feel like they were my friends anymore. When you know someone loves you, it's pretty easy to love them back. But sometimes it's hard to love other people. Sometimes other people are not very lovable.

I stared up at the sky for a while. I drew a picture of a rainbow. Thinking about the rainbow made me miss my friends.

I closed my eyes and wiggled my toes. I picked up my Thinking Book again and turned to the first page. "Choose your thoughts. Choose your life." I turned to the second page: "Does God love me?" *Yes,* I thought, *I know God loves me, and He loves my friends, too.*

I knew just what I needed to do.

"I choose to think about what God says," I said out loud. "I choose to feel loved, and I choose to love others."

Now it's your turn. Tell me about a time when someone hurt your feelings. What did you decide to do?

Something to Think About

Beloved, if God loved us so very much, we also ought to love one another. (1 John 4:11 AB)

In My Own Words

Because God loves me so much, I can love other people.

Something Fun to Do

This could get messy, so make sure you have permission from a grown-up.

1. Grab a plastic bowl and a cup. The cup has to fit inside the bowl, okay?
2. Take the bowl and the cup to the sink.
3. First, put the bowl in the sink. Then put the cup in the bowl.
4. Make sure they are sitting under the faucet.
5. Turn on the water and fill up the cup.
6. Keep running the water until it spills out over the sides of the cup and into the bowl. Go ahead and let it fill up the bowl, but then you have to turn the water off!

Did you see how the water spilled out of the cup and into the bowl when the cup was filled past the top? The water is like God's love. He fills up our hearts with love just like you filled up the cup. What happened when it filled up to the top? It overflowed! The same thing happens when you let God love you. The more you think about how much God loves you, the more His love will fill you up. And the more His love fills you up, the more it will overflow onto the people around you. Pretty cool, huh? Love will just spill right out of you!

Choose Your Thoughts

The next time you are having trouble loving someone, just remember how much God loves you. The more you feel God's love for you, the more you will be able to love other people.

Now It's Your Turn!

Write I John 4:11 in your own words or copy it out of your favorite Bible translation.

Something to Think About

Jesus said, "This is my command: Love each other." (John 15:17 NIV)

In My Own Words

God says we should love each other.

Something Fun to Do

Today, you need some sunglasses. They are going to be your "love glasses." Got 'em? Okay, put them on! Now, walk around your house. Does everything look different? Look in a mirror at yourself. Do you look different?

How we choose to look at things can change what we see. When you put on your love glasses, everything looked different, didn't it? God is always wearing love glasses when He looks at us. He sees us through eyes of love, even when we make mistakes.

How good does it feel to know that God loves you even when you really mess up? How good does it feel when your mom or dad or maybe a friend forgives you when you hurt their feelings? That's why God tells us to love one another! He knows that love always makes things better.

When you're mad at someone, it's hard to be happy, right? All you think about is how mad you are or how much they hurt your feelings, and pretty soon you feel terrible! You forget all about what God says about you and how much He loves you. God's love brings out the best in people. That is why loving someone doesn't mean letting people hurt you or treat you badly—absolutely not! If your friend is bullying you, teasing you, or making you feel badly about yourself, then she isn't much of a friend. God loves you, too, and He doesn't want anyone to hurt you. If someone is hurting you, go back to Lesson 5, quick! But if one of your friends just had a bad day and acted a little rude or bossy, you can think about how much God loves you and how much He loves your friend, and that will help you choose your thoughts. It will help you be able to talk to him or her in a way that makes things better, not worse.

Choose Your Thoughts

The next time someone hurts your feelings, put on your love glasses and see if things look different to you. Choose to think about how much God loves you and what He says about you. God's love will always help you see clearly because it helps you see things from His point of view.

Now It's Your Turn!

Write John 15:17 in your own words or copy it out of your favorite Bible translation.

Something to Think About

Above all, keep fervent in your love for one another, because love covers a multitude of sins. (1 Peter 4:8 NASB)

In My Own Words

If we remember that we love each other, we won't be angry at each other very long when we mess up.

Something Fun to Do

It's time to make a list!

1. Make a list of a few things you've done that probably weren't exactly nice—if you know what I mean. For example, I made a face at my mom when she asked me to put up my shoes. She didn't see it, and I didn't get in trouble. And technically, if you want to be specific, it didn't hurt her feelings because she didn't even know. But I know I did it, and I know it wasn't very nice. So that would go on my list. And maybe the time I had that not-so-nice thought about Grace's story in class. I secretly thought it was a little boring and that mine was better. That would definitely go on my list.
2. Cover the whole list with glue.
3. Then cover the glue in glitter!
4. Shake it off.

What's left? Sparkly, beautiful glitter, right? Well, that's kind of what God's love does to sin. It covers it. Jesus died for every one of us. We all need Him, not just some of us. His love covered every one of our sins. Every time you do something that you know isn't God's best for you, you feel a little farther away from God. All you see is your list of mistakes and failures. But God loves you so much that He will make the most beautiful things out of your mistakes—if you trust Him. When you trust God and trust His love for you, you will listen to His voice. You will follow Him. And because He is so much greater than we are, He will show you how to make beautiful art out of your mess.

Choose Your Thoughts

The next time you get really angry with someone or somebody really hurts your feelings, stop and think about how God loves you even when you mess up. You can cover the other person's mistakes or hurtful behavior with the love of God by remembering that God loves that person too.

Now It's Your Turn!

Write 1 Peter 4:8 in your own words or copy it out of your favorite Bible translation.

Conclusion

Well, here we are at the end of the book! You know exactly how to think now, right? Do you still have questions? That's okay. I do, too. My mom says that we will always have questions. That's just a sign that we are still learning and growing. In John 14:26 NASB, Jesus said, "But the Helper, the Holy Spirit, whom the Father will send in My name, He will teach you all things and bring to your remembrance all that I have said to you."

So don't worry! It's easier than you think! When you ask Jesus to be your Savior, the Holy Spirit comes to live inside of you. Have you done that? Have you asked Jesus to come and live in your heart? There aren't any special words to use, and it doesn't have to be done in any special place. All you have to do is believe that God loves you so much that He sent His Son, Jesus, to take away your sins (all of those mistakes you make when you don't trust God). Then, you ask God to forgive you for trying to do things on your own and messing up. After that, you ask Jesus to come and live in your heart. You tell Him that you want to follow Him. Remember, you don't have to go out and try to be the person God wants you to be; you just have to remember that you *already are* the person God wants you to be! Because of Jesus, you are free from anything that would separate you from God forever. You will always be His child. He will always love you. He will never leave you, no matter what. That means you can trust God with your life. You can trust Him with your choices. That is what choosing your thoughts is all about—learning to choose God's kind of thoughts so you can live God's best life for you!

I'm off to make some more *super important* choices, but I'll see you the next time you stop by. Until then, always choose God's best for you!

P.S.

Right here, right now, as I write this book on how to think, I am perfectly me, Emily, and you are perfectly you. And in case there's no one around to tell you, I want you to know that you are a beautiful picture to the world of God's love and goodness. You have so many gifts and talents. You are blessed, and you are a blessing. God created you on purpose, and He is so proud of you! The God who created the whole world lives in you! He has given you everything He has because He loves you.

And you know what? I do, too!

With love and lots of thoughts worth thinking,
Emily

About the Author

Jolie Wheaton has served as an attorney advocating for the rights of dependent and neglected children. She has also worked with children as a social worker, in children's ministry, and as a dance teacher. In each position, she observed a need for children to live Ephesians 3:16-19, to truly come to know and experience for themselves the love of God.

Jolie admits that she, like Emily, is a dreamer, a thinker, and an asker of curious questions. She lives in Tennessee with the loves of her life—her husband, their children, and of course, their three dogs!